C000228992

chris phipps
namedropper!

Tyne
Bridge
Publishing

© Chris Phipps 2018

Published by
Tyne Bridge Publishing 2018
City Library
Newcastle Upon Tyne
tynebridgepublishing.org.uk

ISBN: 9780951048894

All rights reserved. No part of this book may be reproduced, stored or introduced
into a retreival system or transmitted in any way or by any means (electronic,
mechanical or otherwise) withour prior permission of the publishers.

Layout: David Hepworth
Additional research: Shawn Fairless

Images from the author's collection and Newcastle Libraries
unless otherwise stated.

for diane, for miriam...

...in memory of gary holton.

foreword

A few years ago I was at a North East Film Festival of which I'm the patron. We discussed a post-screening interview with a visiting guest.

"Who will moderate?" I asked, and was told – Chris Phipps.

I then asked who Chris Phipps was and was told – "Oh, he's very good."

They were right, Chris is not just a very good moderator, he is exceptional, as was proved again this year when he chaired a discussion with myself, my partner Dick Clement and director David Batty following a showing of our latest film *My Generation*. He's exceptional, not just because he does his homework, which is easier these days if you plunder Wikipedia, but because he cares so much about his subject, especially if it involves film or music.

Those twin passions are certainly the glue that fortifies our friendship. We usually end up after a couple of drinks in intense discussions, especially involving music trivia. I won't try to compete with Chris on this, he's just too clued in. Yes, I could name the first Kinks' single but Chris could name every track on their debut album. Yes, I know the Proclaimers were the Scottish Everly Brothers but he probably knows where their births are registered.

After all he was a producer of the seminal, coolest of cool rock shows *The Tube*. Apart from that show he has always had a great respect and affection for North Eastern culture and heritage. A true Northern soul - it always surprises me that he has a Brummie accent.

Chris's book is suffused with his customary wit, wisdom and humour. And if Chris Phipps is dropping names, these are names really worth dropping.

Ian La Frenais

introduction

A world-famous Midlands' musician once told me this story - every time he returned home from a world tour his first port of call was his local pub. The regulars greeted him and asked what he had been up to. He began to tell them about stadiums in Japan and America and superstars getting up on stage with him. Within ten minutes he detected that the eyes of his listeners were beginning to glaze over. Before he could finish his story his audience had dispersed muttering 'Namedropper'. He could never quite get over the fact that what he did for a living (and worked very hard for) caused such resentment.

This book is a visual and anecdotal record of my four decades spent in radio and television. I grew up with a passion for film and music and it became my speciality as an interviewer and producer. I faced celebrities with microphones in the BBC radio days of the 70s and then confronted them with cameras from the 80s to the present day for Channel 4 and ITV.

As you will read, it is an extraordinary roll call of names from Madonna to Miles Davis. It is my way of namedropping in the nicest way and I make no apology. If you read between the lines there are production secrets and a record of how music trends and television evolved.

A local newspaper once claimed that I had, 'A personal hotline to the stars'. This bemused me. I don't know, or share the lifestyle of the names on these pages and have never claimed this. These are brief magical encounters with a fragility of fame and all that that entails.

steve broc

early days.

Wolverhampton A 4123

Dudley
A 461

West Bromwich
A 461 (A 4035)
Walsall A 461

k

A 457)

black country correspondent.

'have tape recorder - will travel'.

peter bensimon, steve aynsley, little richard with chris phipps, 1984.

gene vincent *the man with ashtray eyes*

1950s British Rock & Roll television was woeful. *6-5 Special* had all the atmosphere of a youth club supervised by ageing disc jockeys. Most of the performers seemed to wear sweaters or cardigans. Far better were the ITV shows *Drumbeat* and *Oh, Boy*, both produced by Jack Good. These programmes had the advantage of being 'teencentric', rather than appearing to be under adult supervision. Rock & Roll orchestras would back a conveyor belt of guest singers. Marti Wilde looked ludicrous and there was Cliff Richard with crooked teeth and sulky good looks. I first saw real unfettered American Rock & Roll on a music special from Granada TV called *Whole Lotta Shakin'*. It starred the manic Jerry Lee Lewis, the wild Little Richard and an act that would repeatedly satisfy the hunger of British audiences for the genuine American rocker - Gene Vincent. Remember - all the programmes apart from *Whole Lotta Shakin'* only featured British contenders - even Tommy Steele, who launched the first British Rock & Roll tour at the Sunderland Empire, had gone into a highly successful MOR stage musical career.

Gene Vincent, nicknamed 'Crazy Legs', allegedly nearly lost his leg in an accident as a despatch rider, leaving him with a bad limp. This leg anchored his physical performance, rooting him to the spot as he clutched the mike stand and lifted his eyes heavenward to sing in a reedy tone. His biggest hit was *Be Bop A Lula*, rendered with an eerie reverberating echo (I once spoke to his producer, Ken Nelson, who still possessed the tape loop machine that achieved this effect). Like many Rock & Rollers in America, the hits began to dry up and his American career became a diminishing return, but he seemed to lead something of a charmed life as he walked out of the fatal UK car crash that killed Eddie Cochrane.

Vincent's renaissance career in the UK and Europe was aided by none other than TV producer Jack Good. Good, Svengali-like, turned Gene Vincent into a Rock & Roll Richard the Third, clothing him head to foot in black leather with a huge chain and medallion. Vincent would limp onto the stage with Good shouting and bullying him from the wings. Inevitably he was high on pills and booze, partly to relieve the pain of a leg that should have been amputated and was encased in a caliper that protruded over his boots. Stars like Hank Williams and Bela Lugosi had used similar addictive cocktails as sinister panaceas for constant pain.

Suddenly, 'Crazy Legs' Gene Vincent was *actually* near my home in Birmingham! There he was, a living rocker, backed by a group called The Shouts, belting out *Be Bop A Lula* at Bournville Village

Hall. Here was a man screaming about 'white lightning' and 'thunderbird wine' in the heart of a Quaker workers' estate - a 'dry' county where only drinking chocolate was served. It caused quite a stir locally. Two local ladies wrote to the press to say that the performance should have been given an X certificate! His last desperate British tour was captured in a remarkable 1970 BBC documentary entitled *The Rock & Roll Singer*. There were few to meet him at the airport, rehearsal rooms were damp and there was paranoia over pay deadlines as he demanded cash up front before performing. His tour manager was none other than Peter Grant, Led Zeppelin's manager, who would become one of the most feared and respected figures in the music business. This film alerted me to the powerful potential of music documentary and I was determined to become involved at some stage in my career.

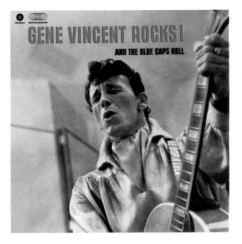

Despite Gene Vincent's extraordinary career, there has never been a dramatisation or feature film of his tragic life. His legacy stylistically, and that of his guitarist Cliff Gallup, are immeasurable. I achieved a small tribute to him on *The Tube* when Vincent aficionado Steve Aynsley, pianist Chas Hodges and Ian Dury performed Dury's eloquent *Sweet Gene Vincent* in Studio 5.

The 'man with the ashtray eyes' would have raised a bottle of Thunderbird to that.

trapeze *coast to coast*

In the early 1970s I managed to get freelance writing work for a rather unique publication - *The Black Country Bugle*, a monthly news publication that is still successfully blowing its own bugle to readers from Stourbridge and Dudley to Wolverhampton and beyond. Perhaps it could be considered a working-class version of *The Dalesman* magazine, a publication to which I have also contributed in more recent years!

The Bugle was the brainchild of its editor Harry Taylor. He served up a mixture of local nostalgia, local history and Black Country dialect stories, most of which he wrote under the pen name Aristotle Tump. For some reason he seemed bent on convincing everyone that Jack the Ripper died in the Black Country - which has never been proved or disproved. Harry felt, as editor, that he should provide some coverage for pop fans, so he gave me a monthly page to fill under the title *Phipps' Forum*. This gave me an entrée into the world of agents and promoters, many of whom I have remained in touch with for decades.

One of the first interviews I secured was with the power trio Trapeze. Hailing from the wider Black Country, Trapeze were a superb funk-edged rock band. With albums like *Medusa*, they had a cult following in the UK, but more importantly found fame on the west coast of America and in Texas. In the photo on the next page I am interviewing Trapeze backstage at Wolverhampton Civic Hall. Just out of shot is Slade drummer Don Powell, who had just survived a near fatal car crash that had killed his fiancée. The photo shows, left to right, Mel Galley, lead guitarist, Glenn Hughes, bass and vocals, Dave Holland, drums. Months and years later this line-up would implode as the different members would be recruited by the giants of the rock world - with varying results. Bassist/vocalist Glenn Hughes once told me that, although he was born in Cannock, his soul came from Detroit. Glenn possessed the most extraordinary blue-eyed soul vocal range. Months after this interview he joined Teessider David Coverdale to front Deep Purple 'Mark 3'. Overcoming a later battle with personal demons, Hughes' voice has graced everyone from Black Sabbath, K.L.F and the hugely successful power trio Black Country Communion. Guitarist Mel Galley later joined Whitesnake, again with David Coverdale in his post-Purple career. Despite a serious accident, Mel continued to play until his untimely death. Dave Holland, drummer, would later join those Midland monsters of rock Judas Priest. Clearly, someone was watching over them that night in Wolverhampton.

trapeze - glenn hughes, mel galley and dave holland with chris phipps (second from left).

black country bugle

9

the drifters *rockin' and driftin'*

The sartorial vocal group The Drifters were four men who sang about worlds far away from my Midland upbringing. They sang about being under the boardwalk, up on the roof, finding sand in their shoes and some places I did know about - the club and the movies on a Saturday night. They were the harbingers of Atlantic Records' Big Beat sound. Their producers married the beat of Rock & Roll with swirling orchestral strings plus a hint of Latin American. Indeed, the Drifters' *Save The Last Dance for Me* was originally intended to provide the finale for the cult movie *Dirty Dancing*.

At my first encounter with The Drifters I was seriously short changed. The act billed as 'The Drifters USA' that bounded on stage at The Crazy E Club in Birmingham were clearly not American and not The Drifters. To make matters worse, they sang a Temptations number! An unscrupulous promoter was passing off a bogus line-up as both classic American soul groups.

I managed to catch up with the genuine - or near original - line-up of The Drifters when I interviewed them at the Wolverhampton Gaumont in 1973. On the bill was Major Lance, who is today a Northern soul icon, and perhaps remembered more than Wayne Fontana who charted with a cover of Lance's classic *Um Um Um*. In the dressing room with The Drifters was the widow of their manager Guy Treadwell. She told me in no uncertain terms that the copyright, name and line-up of the group were heavily protected to prevent experiences such as I had had several years earlier. I was so enthusiastic in my interview that I forgot the time and Johnny Moore said to me, 'Man, are you writing a book or doing an interview?' The official Drifters tour to this day, still emerging from under that boardwalk.

THE POLICE
*WOULD BE GREATLY OBLIGED TO
MEMBERS IF THEY WOULD KEEP*
DRESSING ROOM
WINDOWS *CLOSED*
AS FAR AS POSSIBLE

chris phipps with
johnny moore.

captain beefheart *do i look like salvador dali?*

Captain Beefheart, usually accompanied by his Magic Band, was the stage persona of performance artist Don Van Vliet. Critics were bitterly divided over his music, which was championed on Radio 1 by John 'Monotone' Peel. When I put on his *Safe As Milk* album in a common room, I was pelted with biscuits. Most people, it seemed, wanted the ersatz soul of Geno Washington.

Beefheart to me was a musical version of pop art. He sang like Howling Wolf on speed in what I can only describe as a 'Dracula vibrato'. His song titles included *Willie the Pimp*, *Electricity* and *Beatle Bones and Rolling Stones*. Oh, yes, he hung out with Frank Zappa, brandishing a vacuum cylinder cleaner in a gate-fold sleeve album cover. He was both alienating and bewildering, just on the right side of pretentious.

When, as a journalist, I awaited him on his tour coach at Lanchester College. Also on board was a Mother of Invention, Jimmy Carl Black (whose nickname was Motorhead), and Zoot Horn Rollo on guitar!

During the interview I learned a very sharp lesson - never make assumptions about your subject and never get smart. The album I was interviewing him about contained the track *Dali's Car* and I quite flippantly asked, 'Are you a musical version of Salvador Dali?' At this he lunged forward to about a tenth of an inch from my face and said furiously, 'Do I look like F***** Salvador Dali? F**** off this bus NOW 'cos I'm F****** paying for it!!' We patched things up later and he became very expansive about his art, but in that moment I had nearly blown it.

When I watched his performance on The Old Grey Whistle Test the following week I have to confess that a mild shudder went through me - I'd had a sobering experience.

Ironically, the interview was published in *The Black Country Bugle* opposite Pub of the Month. I remember a petrol station attendant in Dudley, who was well into underground music, telling me he couldn't quite believe his eyes when he was confronted by the sight of ol' Beefheart in *The Bugle!* Neither could I, and he continued to confound for years to come.

the captain!

frankie miller *a fool in love*

Barbarella's was a nightclub near Broad Street in Birmingham. It was as if Roger Vadim had attempted to land in the Midlands with a style statement. It was a labyrinth of chrome and neon, boasting rooms with names like 'Date a Chic'. Unwittingly, it became a prime music venue for rising and visiting bands. Here was a chance to see Curtis Mayfield, The Chi Lites, Horslips, The Specials, Selecter and AC/DC. Regulars were Gary Holton's Heavy Metal Kids, whose roadies were constantly accused of stealing chicken from the barbecue. Kevin Rowland's pre-Dexy's band The Killjoys only got through two numbers before the entire club erupted into one of the biggest fights I have ever seen.

It was a regular venue for radio interviews. A memorable one was with a groupie-turned-vocalist called Cherry Vanilla. She gave a great interview, but I had to leave to edit it for the rock show and never saw her perform. If I had stayed I would have seen a very early performance by The Police who were her backing band for the British tour. It would have been easy for me to pretend that I had seen them!

The photograph shows one of the greatest vocalists we have ever produced - Frankie Miller. This Glaswegian was gifted with a voice somewhere between Paul Rodgers and Joe Cocker. It is said that the only difference between Rod Stewart and Frankie Miller was a bottle of hair bleach. The interview was in support of an album entitled *The Rock*. He told me about his wanderings in the shipyards of Glasgow and the levees of New Orleans, which inspired much of his song writing. He met a man who threw his coat into the river and turned to him and said 'I'd do the same with myself but I haven't got the guts' and this inspired one of his songs. It is said that Otis Redding's widow openly wept when she heard Frankie's voice.

chris phipps with frankie miller.

uriah heep *very 'umble*

My very first radio rock band interview was with burgeoning prog-rockers Uriah Heep. I first saw Uriah Heep at Birmingham Town Hall, supporting the incredible American nostalgia Rock & Roll act Sha Na Na. The Heep, as they were known, were quite an odd contrast to the headliners - the line-up included guitarist Mick Box, moustachioed vocalist David Byron and Hammond organ thunderer and composer Ken Hensley. Their material ranged from riff-laden ballads like *Gypsy* to great slabs of swirling organ opuses like *Salisbury*. I secured an interview when they released the album *Return to Fantasy*. The band, I was told, would be in their room at the Holiday Inn in Birmingham. Armed with a portable tape recorder on my shoulder, I could hear the sound of my feet echoing down the hotel corridor as I knocked nervously on the door. When the door opened there was the entire band plus their entourage sitting in a semi-circle in front of me, with their manager and record label owner Gerry Bron, who sat like the Dali Lama in the middle. He fixed me with a stare and asked what I was doing to promote the album. 'This interview,' I curtly replied and somehow managed to get through it by mainly talking to Ken Hensley. After the interview I was joined in the lift by vocalist David Byron. I said to him that I had felt very nervous. He replied, 'Don't forget we are nervous too.' I have never forgotten that advice and it has helped me a lot. *...Very 'Eavy ...Very 'Umble*, as their first album was appropriately titled!

bob marley *steppin' razor*

The Midlands in the 1970s were a cultural pressure cooker ever ready to blow. It was a giant mixing board of home-grown and imported musical roots. This was a situation that could erupt either into street violence and riots or into creative musical outpourings. Coventry blew up into the 2Tone explosion, bands like The Specials and The Selecter fused Ska (reggae's predecessor) with punk sentiments. In the Birmingham suburb of Handsworth, Steel Pulse issued one of the most important reggae albums ever made - *Handsworth Revolution*.

Inevitably, local radio and television broadcasting based at BBC Pebble Mill would become an unintentional mirror for this revolution. Every Tuesday night in the regional opt-out slot, when the BBC went local, there was an arts/music programme called *Look! Hear!* I was cast in the presenter role as Midland TV's answer to Keith Chegwin, a foil in the studio to Toyah Willcox, who we had hired at the premiere of Derek Jarman's punk movie *Jubilee*. This was a smart move as she was bound for the charts and screen with a very high profile. It was the music that really counted, captured in Studio 1 at BBC Pebble Mill. Steel Pulse performed *Handsworth Revolution* dressed in Ku Klux Klan outfits. The Selecter, performing *Too Much Pressure*, encouraged a stage invasion by fans whose pogoing resulted in the collapse of the platform. I felt that the more staid factions at the BBC were freaked out by all this apparent anarchy we were bringing in - good! Other fine bands who performed included Eclipse and Weapons of Peace. There was always the hope that UB40 would perform but I knew that they never would. They were extremely shrewd in controlling their public profile. Their mix of urban-inspired reggae, particularly their crate digging for original cover versions, would mean that they would become the biggest selling reggae pop act in the world. Many Jamaican artists who would otherwise languish in poverty would owe their pensions to UB40's version of their song. In terms of broadcasting, Chris Blackwell's Island Records and Richard Branson's Virgin Records really knew how to distribute and handle reggae music as a commodity. Dealing with reggae in a business sense is a whole different ball game. Be prepared to tear up the rule book! I would develop a long relationship with Island Records and even occasionally met its founder Chris Blackwell in the most unlikely places. Amongst his incredible A&R achievements, which include signing U2, he is responsible for signing and marketing Bob Marley. It was a shrewd move taking Marley and The Wailers from their native Jamaica and marketing them like a 1970s rock band.

I first heard Bob Marley when I reviewed his album *African Herbsman*, which was on the pre-Island Trojan label. I saw him perform at Stafford Bingley Hall, a Midlands venue that was literally a cattle shed. Marley's lion-like stance on stage and his political statements had a real effect. I hadn't seen such a potent mix of politics and music since witnessing Nina Simone at Birmingham Town Hall when she encored with her version of *Young, Gifted and Black* with a rose tucked into her leather boots.

In 1991 Channel 4 commissioned a tenth anniversary documentary entitled *Bob Marley - Time Will Tell*. I was given the challenge of structuring an documentary almost impossible to make. The problem is that paying tribute to Bob Marley, like John Lennon, means that, as many people deify him, the editorial balance of the contributions can be seriously affected and almost hysterical. We took the radical decision not to interview anyone about him and use only *his* words gleaned from radio and film interviews to tell his own life story. I was given a toolbox that contained every audio interview he ever did. These were transcribed and then edited/spliced for weeks to form a personal ninety minute autobiographical narrative. Using only speech narration meant we could screen uninterrupted performances by Bob Marley obtained from archives all over the world. We even found overexposed footage of Bob Marley nursing his injuries after an assassination attempt. He had taken refuge in what were colonial tea rooms, which today are one of the world's most exclusive hotels. My last meeting with Chris Blackwell was, in fact, in the dusty room of that building before it was converted. The documentary was directed by Declan Lowney and is now regarded as a milestone in archive narrative documentary making. My only regret was that a version of *No Woman No Cry*, recorded live at the Amandla concert in Boston could not be included at the time.

marley - the young lion.

from under the smoke

This remarkable picture is of myself and the characterful Bill Cattell. Bill was a Black Country publican who, as you can see, was a champion among pigeon racers and fanciers. His lofts were next to the pub that he kept - The New Inns on the Wolverhampton Road out of Birmingham. I am wielding a UHER tape recorder, from which I derived a living as a freelance reporter for nearly ten years. My main task was to compile and present a weekly radio magazine programme called *Wulfrun Echo*, which covered the Black Country area of the West Midlands. Bill was a regular contributor to the programme as he gave out the pigeon racing results. Other regular contributors were the Black Country poet and writer Jim William Jones, historian Keith Gayle and Cannock historian Reg Fullelove. Of course, much of the programme was in Black Country dialect and some hardliners viewed me as an interloping Brummie outsider. They did not know that my father was a Black Country man from Tipton.

Wulfrun Echo beamed out from BBC Radio Birmingham for nearly ten years. The signature tune was a rousing brass band composition, *Two Marching Sergeants*. The programme epitomises local radio production - I was meeting and interviewing individuals who had never been in front of a microphone before. Many interviewees were witnesses to a flourishing, then declining, regional industrial heritage going back to the beginning of the century. I unwittingly recorded memories of times that were all but vanished by the 1970s. There was a chain maker, a confectioner, a woman who made nails (by hand) for a living in Halesowen and an octogenarian who had helped to forge the storm anchors for the *Titanic*. Equally memorable, I accompanied cart owners and even an old pram owner who made a living from 'totting' (collecting scrap) round the streets of Dudley and Netherton, plus cobblers, organ builders and canal labourers.

Some stories were sold on to the BBC network. Two of the most extraordinary ones were two bus drivers who had recreated World War One tank warfare in their back garden and a woman in Darlaston who ran a coal-fired fish & chip shop from a former cow shed. Needless to say, items like this would find their way onto the *John Dunne Show* and *Woman's Hour*. I am happy to say that the best of these interviews survive today in history archives in Dudley, records of a lost working class culture and hard-won pride.

BBC Radio Birmingham eventually got a makeover and was renamed Radio WM, numbering the late Ed Doolan among its presenters. I always felt that BBC local radio in the 70s, unlike its commercial opponent, was too compartmentalised in its output, yet without it, these incredible memories would never have been captured.

looking west - bill cattell and chris phipps.

willoughby GUS gullachsen

link wray *rumblin' and rockin'*

Sixty years ago, in 1958, an instrumental record changed the world for ever. It was called *Rumble*. It sounded, as it came out of the speakers, as though it was predatory and stalking you, as it shivered and swaggered in a sea of feedback. It was performed by Link Wray, a guitarist who had recorded it and many other threateningly-titled works on a three track studio in a converted chicken coop. *Rumble* seemed to distill a whole teenage exploitation movie into two and a half minutes. It was so threatening that it was banned for inciting juvenile delinquency. It is arguable that Pete Townsend, Ray and Dave Davies and Jimmy Page were partly inspired to take up the axe as a result of the record. It is the ultimate riff.

In 1970 Link Wray turned up in Birmingham in the company of vocalist Robert Gordon to play a gig at Barbarella's club in the city centre. I managed to get an interview and was confronted by a man who I can only describe as looking like a cross between Elvis Presley and Roy Orbison. He spoke to me with that wonderful Southern finesse that comes from Tennessee and Louisiana. What follows is a transcript of the short interview made over forty years ago.

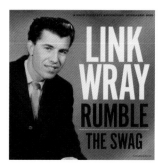

You're known for the song Rumble, is it an albatross around your neck?

A disc jockey told me that in 1957, and that's before I ever recorded it. I was just playing it around shows and record hops and he told me, Lenny you will never out live that song. I said I hope you are wrong. He wasn't wrong. It's the biggest song I have ever had in my life, I have cut many albums I have cut many instrumentals, I have cut many songs and I have had a lot of hits, but nothing as big as *Rumble*.

Why do you think it has become so legendary?

It's influenced so many people like Pete Townsend for instance of the Who. Well they were kids, Pete was about twelve or thirteen when *Rumble* came out. *Rumble* has got three chords, it's got a D Chord and it's got an E chord. You can learn off *Rumble* it is so simple. I think the simplest things in life are the greatest and me and Hank Williams proved that. You can take jazz and they can take one chord and make many notes

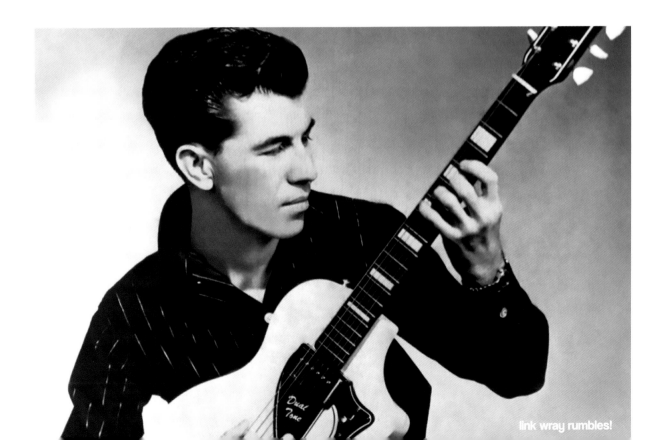

link wray rumbles!

Do you think we have got away from this basic sound in the past few years and do you think you are returning to it now?

I don't think I got away from it - I think it got away from me.

You have a basic, primitive sound which I think appeals to people, do you agree with that?

Yes, I agree I play simple, I play with feeling, whereas Pete Townsend is a better guitar player than me but he is a very technical player, he is a genius. I just play with feeling. I think the music has gotten back around to me again this year. This new wave music is nothing but old time rock & roll. It has gotten back to drums, bass, and guitar and kids are out there shouting out like they did with the Ramones and The Sex Pistols. If you like one, you will like all of them. They aren't called by technical chords, technical runs, it's just feeling, and the kids are picking up on that.

You have joined up with Robert so successfully over the past two years it comes as a surprise to many people that you have been very reluctant to record at certain times haven't you?

Well it's all on account to big record business and there an awful lot of crooks out there and are still out there you know. They steal a lot of money. I have had a lot of money stolen off me. I have been ripped off right left and centre but I'm still here

playing music, I'm still here, I'm still happy, I'm not a rich man but I'm still happy, I have a wife and three kids.

Have you still got the recording shack?

No, we got rid of that. It was a chicken coop you know. We were recording in the basement of my brother's house on the farm. His wife worked for the government and she told me that he had to take his recording place somewhere else, so he took it out and put it in the chicken coop, and that's where we recorded the Shack Album for Polydor. But that's another road I have travelled you know but it's still with my roots.

Let's get back to the road you are travelling now. Robert we have totally left you out until now. The first thing I want to ask you is about the liner notes of the album and what you said to the press, you aren't just merely reviving rock & roll you are living it, you are singing it for what it is.

That's true. I'm not a revival act, this is the music I have always really dug, and that's why I do it you know. I think anything I sing comes out with this kind of feeling you know, whether it is an old tune or a new tune like one at Link Road on the new record that is coming out. Link's brother Doug wrote a tune that we are doing on the record and the Springsteen song we did tonight, it just comes off with that kind of feel, and it's just the kind of music I have always listened to.

Why do you think it lasts? because it's basic? because it deals with just straight honest issues? like hurt and love?

I guess so - and also it's vocal it's not screaming and it's not yelling any kind of political kind of bullshit. Its just straight ahead. I'm not trying to make any statements or anything, I'm just singing songs that people can relate to.

And enjoy!

That's right.

Link said why he likes playing with you but why do you like playing at the front with Link? I know you feel embarrassed but try and tell me.

No, I don't feel embarrassed at all man. Link is really an inspiration to anybody that plays with him and anybody that works with him. For me it adds a real authenticity to the type of music I am doing. Also because I happen to really dig the guy.

alamy

clash *of the* luvvies

In the 1970s, as a producer at BBC Pebble Mill, I found myself on the regular book publicisty circuit slated to interview celebrities for radio prior to them appearing on *Pebble Mill At One*. Publicists would send me a copy of the book in advance, and anticipating that I wouldn't read it, a list of pre-prepared questions. Where possible, I would try and read some or all of the book. The one thing that you never did was say to your guest that you had read the book when you hadn't, they would always know.

James Mason, with his dark looks and rasping voice, had gone from Huddersfield to Hollywood super stardom. For many, even today, he is the ultimate Captain Nemo. Initially, I found him aloof, but he eventually warmed, particularly when I mentioned his acting debut at a small theatre in the heart of the Midlands' Black Country. His agent sent me a note to say how much he had enjoyed the interview. I detected that he, like many classic actors, treated television with disdain, despite the fact that he made a great impression in *Salem's Lot*, acting opposite David Soul.

John Mills was both dapper and surprisingly dull, though many actors are and that is why they transform in character. He seemed not to want to admit any failure in his career. I asked him what had been his biggest disappointment, to which he replied *African Queen*. I told him that he wasn't in that film - and he said that is why he was disappointed. John Mills embraced television, playing one of my favourite characters, Professor Quatermass, who saved us from aliens over the years. *Quatermass* creator Nigel Kneale told me he categorically wasn't a science fiction writer, didn't like *Doctor Who* and hated the actor chosen to play Quatermass in the Hammer film series. He told me that actor Brian Donlevy was too tubby and spent all his time chasing his hairpiece!

Albert Finney had a daunting physical presence, yet when I interviewed him, when he was playing Hamlet and later Daddy Worbucks in the film *Annie*, he really put me at my ease and unusually, rather than plugging the performance in hand, willingly talked about his career. He was particularly interesting on the subject of a film called *Wolfen*, a somewhat overlooked role and film which is an unusual mixture of ecology and horror. Finney was attending the premiere of *Annie* when I interviewed him and I got the bonus of interviewing its director, the Hollywood veteran John Huston. I couldn't believe my luck because here was the man who had directed Bogart and Bacall in classic film noir. At the time of the interview there was a chart record out called *Key Largo*, so I asked Huston what Bogart would have thought of such a thing. He told me that Bogart would have loved it. He also told me that Bogart was the only actor who didn't need a gun to look threatening.

The biggest Hollywood star I was confronted by was Jane Fonda, and in most unusual circumstances. Her name came up on the list on a Sunday afternoon news reporting shift. She was in Birmingham with her political hat on to promote awareness of the plight of the Californian grape farmers. Ironically her father, Henry Fonda, had played a grape farmer in the movie *Grapes of Wrath*. So, on a rainy Sunday afternoon, in the cold unforgiving atmosphere of a deserted City Hall in Birmingham city centre there sat *Barbarella* herself next to the tea urn and copies of *The Socialist Weekly*. I never quite lived it down and a voice in my head kept saying 'It isn't really Jane Fonda, is it?'

Her interview, and address to a small audience, was eloquent and inspiring on a shift whose normal high spot was a Jaguar factory walk out in Coventry.

Inevitably I found myself in many dressing rooms. Marlene Dietrich, in Wolverhampton, only granted a short interview about the songs she was about to perform. She resolutely refused to talk about her films and fixed me with her hooded eyes.

Peter Wyngarde, who I interviewed in Wolverhampton Grand Theatre, was playing Dracula opposite Nyree Dawn Porter. Because he was looking into his dressing room mirror, I had to hold the microphone at an angle in front of him. In so doing, I knocked over a framed picture of his mentor, the actress Margaret Leighton. He was distraught. A fortnight later he was involved in an unfortunate incident in a Gloucester public lavatory. Peter of course had been the flamboyant Jason King and I'm glad to say that he achieved cult status in Mike Hodges' high camp *Flash Gordon*.

chris phipps interviewing
albert finney, chelsea hotel.

From Anne Groves

Publicity department

Dear Chris –

I've been trying to get through on the phone since Friday with no success – so I thought I must drop you a line to say thank you very much indeed for what was probably the best interview in the whole of James Mason's publicity tour. He [Mason] was very impressed – and enjoyed the interview because of your enthusiasm and your thorough knowledge of the book.

Thanks again – and see you soon I hope.

Yours, Anne Groves.

Another actor who insisted on maintaining his profile when being interviewed was Nicol Williamson. It was on the set of the Sherlock Holmes movie *The Seven Per Cent Solution*. The location was the Severn Valley Railway and I was kept waiting two hours outside his caravan. He did have the good grace to apologise. He is the only actor to play Hamlet with a Birmingham accent.

Finally, we have a picture of the legendary movie animator, the genius of stop motion, Ray Harryhausen with his mechanical owl, Bubo, from *Clash of the Titans*. Harryhausen was in love with his art and his attention to detail and devotion to painstakingly adjusting armatures in front of the camera endeared his work to audiences all over the world. This modest man injected his own humanity into everything he created. In the face of CGI and incredible special effects used today there is still no substitute for the battling skeletons he created to confront Jason in *Jason and the Argonauts*. There has been a remake of *Clash of the Titans*, but they didn't get near the mechanical owl. As the critic Gary Giddens told me, even when you work out how Ray Harryhausen did it we still don't care because it is magic.

My only disappointment in this run of interviews was a cancellation on the part of Sammy Davis Junior, who pulled out of his book tour. I was lucky enough to see him perform at the London Palladium in 1978. A true master, who I think is overlooked today. As James Brown said, 'Maybe he was too good at too many things.'

loughby GUS gullachsen

'don't look at the medusa!' ray harryhausen and chris phipps.

kinky boots a matter of honor

The expression 'They should have known better', applies to those members of the acting profession whose overzealous agents convinced them that stardom on the screen can transfer to stardom on vinyl. The mistakes committed in the name of recording are too numerous to mention. They include Rudolf Valentino, Anthony Perkins, Dirk Bogarde, Telly Savalas, William Shatner and even Jack Howarth from *Coronation Street* who put out an album of Lancashire monologues. On rare occasions the results were startlingly good as in the case of Robert Mitchum's calypso albums. Needless to say, such quality was extremely rare.

Honor Blackman, a Rank starlet, had led a fairly undistinguished screen career in British movies until the advent of *The Avengers*. Blackman played the leather clad Cathy Gayle, a feisty foil to John Steed, the enigmatic and urbane agent played by Patrick MacNee. Prior to *The Avengers* women in action series had played molls or secretaries cowering and making tea. Cathy Gayle ushered in a new era of powerful women hurtling male opponents across the set with her martial arts skills. She propelled the series into cult status.

Inevitably, Gayle and Steed entered the recording studio. They had a whimsical hit based on Cathy's fashion statement, her 'kinky boots'.

Honor Blackman then made a solo album entitled *Everything I've Got*. There she is on the sleeve in front of a Rolls Royce *and* a private plane. I found this kitch treasure in a charity shop box along with a Julie London album and the equally bonkers *Elizabeth Taylor in London*!

Ironically, I don't collect autographs and never have. I just had to make an exception and get Honor's signature on the sleeve of her record.

Approaching seventy, she appeared in a one woman show at the Tyne Theatre and Opera House in Newcastle. There, slightly trembling, I proffered it to her when we met in her dressing room. She looked at me and asked in that voice similar in tone to Joan Greenwood and Fenella Fielding, 'Young man are you quite mad!' My reply was that yes I was quite mad.

honor blackman -
'are you quite
mad?'

mr ulrich, *i presume?*

In the late 1970s a music revolution emerged under the title NWOBHM - the New Wave of British Heavy Metal. Young, in some cases very young, aspiring metal bands assumed a DIY directness in the new style of heavy metal that they performed. Many recorded low-budget EPs or albums, which were on independent labels and distributed through independent distributors. The sound and the style was stripped back, full of energy and clearly ripping off the punk ethic. Inevitably major labels hoovered up the most likely candidates with varying results. The most enduring acts became Iron Maiden and Def Leppard, who ultimately found major success in America and beyond.

Serious contenders were a Black Country quartet from Stourbridge called Diamond Head. Vocalist Sean Harris and guitarist Brian Tatler achieved an incredible chemistry that I witnessed at a local village hall. I managed to get them a slot on *Look! Hear!* The band asked me to DJ live and introduce them on stage on a number of occasions. In Herefordshire we found ourselves at an extraordinary Art Deco ballroom, seemingly in the middle of nowhere. It had a bit of a David Lynch *Twin Peaks* feel about it. The support band were called Hamburger Mary and they had a one-legged drummer with a highly decorated prosthetic leg.

The meagre audience numbered a few local bikers and the ballroom owner was clearly perplexed by the whole evening. Now comes the real point of this story. As I was setting up my DJ equipment and opening my record boxes, I was approached by an American teenager clad in denim with a shock of blonde hair. It seemed that he had travelled a long way for this gig to see his heroes. He politely asked me whether I could sell or give him a single entitled *Hooker Hater* by a band called Demolition. I thought - 'if he's come all this distance he can have it for free and I could get another promo copy anyway'. Yes, you may have guessed, this young fan from America was none other than Metallica's drummer Lars Ulrich, though I never asked him his name. It is now verified in definitive biographies that he was at the Hereford gig, such was his admiration for their sound. Metallica would eventually pay homage to Diamond Head by covering some of their classic tracks. This is true vindication of the band who, despite a deal with MCA records, never delivered their initial potential. Brian Tatler still tours his version of Diamond Head to this day. The single I gave to young Lars is currently worth three to four hundred pounds - So can I have it back?

chris phipps with toyah willcox and roger casstles on the set of look! hear!

willoughby GUS gullachsen

DIAM∧ND HEAD

PETER BATES
MANAGEMENT &
COLESHILL, BIRN
ENGLAND
Telephone: COLE!

twisted sister we're not gonna take it!

An official book about *The Tube* states that I first saw Twisted Sister in a downtown bar in New York. Wrong! I discovered them (along with twenty thousand other people) at Reading Festival in 1982. What blew me away about them was their finely honed theatricality. Twisted Sister were a collision of Glam Rock, Heavy Metal and Burlesque. The focus of the act was front man Dee Snider, who looked like the progeny of Widow Twanky and Frank N. Furter. The towering Snider took no prisoners in their confrontational live performances.

In 1982, I knew that I would be booking for the *The Tube*, which beamed out from Tyne Tees Television Studio 5 on City Road, Newcastle every Friday at 5.30pm. I knew that this band wowing the crowd at Reading would make for great live television. Their manager told me that if I could secure them a slot they would finance their own trip to the UK and honour it. At this time, remember, they were not with a major record company, so there was a financial risk involved. True to their word, they arrived one Thursday in October outside *The Tube* studio entrance in a Commer van. As they strode through the entrance and into the studio, even without their makeup, they looked pretty daunting. A number of staff suddenly took their lunch breaks early. Their cover was slightly blown when one member of the band known as Mark 'The Animal' Mendoza asked me for a copy of the *Sunday Times* so he could do the crossword. It was also rumoured that somewhere under the greasepaint and the muscle there were degrees in fine arts.

On the Friday night Twisted Sister blew Studio 5 apart, Snider deftly avoiding any expletives. As a bonus they encored with The Rolling Stones *It's Only Rock and Roll*, joined by Lemmy and Brian from Motorhead.

In the audience was Atlantic Records' Phil Carson, who had brought up Foreigner's Mick Jones as a guest. The following day Carson signed Twisted Sister to Atlantic Records and the rest, as they say, is chart and rock history. The late Paula Yates always linked me inextricably with Twisted Sister coming into the world as though it were my fault. The live performance, along with U2 at Red Rocks, remained the favourite performance for director Gavin Taylor.

twisted sister - attitude!

sting *angel of light*

The photograph opposite is a crew shot taken at the inauguration of Newcastle College by Sting. This event and the subsequent Variety Club dinner held in his honour formed the basis of a documentary called *Sting, An Unlikely Lad*, which I produced. At any event stars like this are closely protected by their management. I was told in no uncertain terms that I would get four minutes with him. In fact I got thirty because I locked his management out of the studio. He didn't care.

This wasn't the first time that I had interviewed Sting. We go back to the late 1970s and a director called Alastair Reid. Alastair was one of British film and television's overlooked directors. We struck up a friendship at BBC Birmingham. His career began when he directed *Emergency Ward Ten*, an early live soap where the scenery often vanished behind the actors. He also directed *Baby Love* - an exploitation movie. The producer paid him a thousand pounds and gave him a new suit because he was deemed too scruffy to turn up to the premiere.

In Birmingham he was directing *Gangsters*. This was a mould-breaking 1970s' drama series written by Philip Martin. It was unusual in many ways. The plot revolved around an ex-SAS man called Klein who worked undercover in the dark underworld that was for once, not the East End of London, but Birmingham. It began as a TV movie which

spawned two series. For the first time (using high speed cameras) cars weren't racing round New York, they were racing round Spaghetti Junction - and the cast was multicultural, including Paul Barber and the future butler in *The Fresh Prince of Bel Air*. The two television series, under Alastair's direction, became more and more surreal. Klein was injured in one episode and was rescued by none other than Dan Archer in a simultaneous radio episode on the week of transmission. There was also a wonderful parody of a Kung Fu movie filmed in Birmingham City Centre. To top it all Alastair put a touch of Hitchcock cameo into the proceedings by appearing himself as a grave digger. I supplied some of the locations for *Gangsters*, including a little known area of catacombs in Birmingham's Jewellery Quarter.

Whither Sting? Alastair's next project was *Artemis 81*. This was a marathon drama, which to this day, rather like Raymond Chandler's *The Big Sleep*, no one really understands, including Alastair himself. The cast included Gudrun Ure, who would become famous as *Supergran,* and Hollywood heavy Stirling Hayden. Hayden had been the star of the classic film noir *The Asphalt Jungle*. He told me that the only reason he ever acted was to finance his life on the ocean wave, because he was happier at sea. This interview has unfortunately been lost. The locations included a Swiss lake and an underground hydroelectric station. The most spectacular was Crich Tramway Museum in the Midlands which was transformed into an Eastern European border post where the entire population had been gassed!

It remains the longest tracking shot on British television. Amongst the dead walks Helix, the angel of light, played, you guessed it, by Sting.

Alastair tipped me off that I could get an exclusive interview with Sting on the set if I turned up.

With some trepidation, I asked Sting, who was seated in a cramped location coach, whether it was difficult to be taken seriously as an actor when you are a rock star. I didn't feel that he was helpful during the interview, but I got what I wanted anyway. The exclusivity of the interview got it a network airing and a lot of local journalists who never gave me the time of day were suddenly ringing me to get details of the interview for their own bylines. I was working for local radio at the time and their newspapers supported commercial radio, yet they had never given me any previous publicity. My response to them would not be suitable for this book.

Alastair Reid would go on to direct *Tales From the City* and *Traffik*. True to form, there he was, a conductor on a San Francisco tram - Hitchcockian to the end.

jenny brewer

37

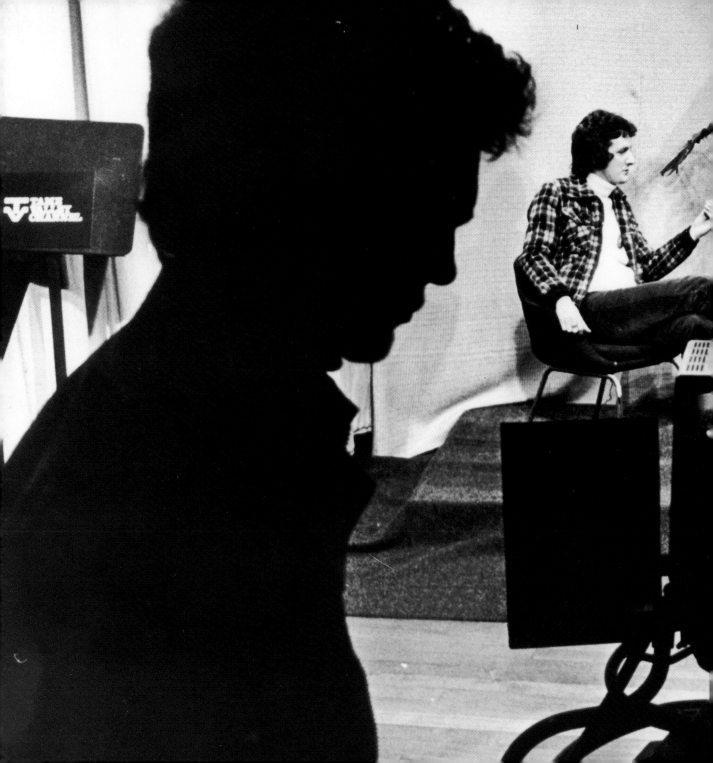

grace jones *pull up to the bumper*

Here's Grace Jones in a Mickey Mouse hat. The venue was Birmingham Botanical Gardens in October 1982, a rainy Sunday afternoon.

We had filmed interviews that week in the Midlands for *The Tube* including Robert Plant in Dudley. In performance we got The Maisonettes and punk maestros Charged GBH. The latter were filmed on the roof of Birmingham Central Fire Station performing appropriately *Gimme Fire* - concluding with a gas canister that failed to ignite - who said Health & Safety?

Grace Jones had a reputation with TV interviewers, including slapping Russell Harty. No such luck for Jools Holland - his opening question to our Grace was 'Who would you have liked to have worked with who's dead?' Game over.

I met her once more in Ibiza for a TV special - she was charming.

next page) chris phipps looking cautious with grace jones.

robert plant *burning down one side*

JBS was an uninteresting looking brick hut on the outskirts of Dudley. But its interior was a venue for very important gigs in the history of the Midlands' Black Country. I first saw an act called Darts there. For me they were the best Rock & Roll parody act outside Sha Na Na - and they were British. One of the two vocalists was a bug-eyed clown called Den Hegarty. He eventually became a presenter for Tyne Tees Television on their classic rock series *All Right Now*. The club had a security man/DJ called 'Jimmy The Con'. His repertoire as a DJ included Holst's *Mars: The Bringer of War*. I filmed two bands at JBS for *The Tube* - The Maisonettes who charted with *Heartache Avenue* which for me was a clever pastiche of Motown.

The photographs opposite, taken in 1982, feature Robert Plant. I first saw him at The Midlands Arts Centre in Birmingham. He got up to sing at the invitation of Alexis Korner. I didn't know who he was but I remembered his pinstriped suit, his physicality and the power of his vocals. Of course he and fellow Midlander John Bonham would complete the line-up of the New Yardbirds, in turn, destined to become Led Zeppelin. This band would evolve and transform Rock & Roll, Doo Wop, R&B, blues and folk into a new devastating legacy. The key to Led Zeppelin was enigma - no singles, interviews, TV performances and often no album credits. On stage they were loose cannons - Bonham, Celtic hippie Plant, androgynous Page and scholarly Jones. They engendered a 'whole lotta' rumours too.

The last Led Zeppelin performance I saw was Knebworth in 1978. There was an initial nervousness in the performance and a strange silence hanging over the festival and its surroundings. The band's power however was undeniable. In 1982 I produced Robert Plant's first post-Zeppelin interview in support of his solo album. It must have been difficult for him to cross over from enigma to exposure but the interview with *Tube* presenter Jools Holland was very candid and not hesitant.

One reason for the success of this interview was the use of JBS club as a venue. Robert Plant had a musical alter-ego away from the stadiums. This was a steaming chitlin' circuit, R&B band called The Honeydrippers. With this line up he curated a set list of R&B classics which he had served up at least twice at this venue - so he felt at home at JBS. The second reason for the interview's success was Jools Holland. He was the perfect foil. His musical credibility plus his idiosyncratic questions were his mastercards.

Robert Plant's search for and reinterpretation of his roots and influences have vindicated him time and time again with grammy award winning results.

The endless rumour mill of 'Will they won't they?' was satiated at Led Zeppelin's O2 reunion. This eventually emerged on the screen as Dick Carruther's *Celebration Day* on which I worked very briefly. It would have been so easy for that circus to continue but it didn't - but with Led Zeppelin you never say never.

robert plant with jools holland, 1982

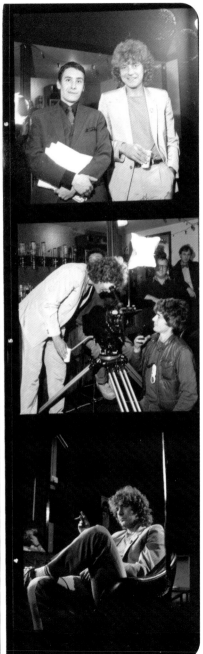

tina turner *let's stay together*

I guess if you were sat on Tina Turner's knee (pictured right) you would be smiling as well. It is really a smile of achievement, as Tina Turner's appearance on *The Tube* was probably the most important television booking I ever made. I had seen Ike and Tina Turner Revue in Birmingham at a club called The Crazy E, which, I think, doubled as The Harp Club. It was a great show, particularly The Ikettes whose name embodied Ike Turner's ruthless operation of the band. As his eventual autobiography would reveal, he put his name on everything and everybody like a burning brand. I also remember they sported a bright orange sound system.

In 1981 in New York I saw two legendary acts, both with the surname Turner. There was Big Joe Turner, the original blues shouter whose career had a Rock & Roll cross-over element even before Rock & Roll was conjured as a name by D.J. Alan Freed. I loved Big Joe and had all his LPs, now here he was - immaculate in a double-breasted suit, beaming at me, hauling his giant frame up on stage at Tracks club to belt out everything from *Corinna, Corinna* to *Shake, Rattle and Roll*. He just sat there on a bar chair, backed by a trio, and blew everybody away. It probably was one of his last performances.

At The Ritz in downtown New York, which seemed to be a ballroom that had seen better days, I went to see Tina Turner. What I saw took me completely by surprise. Sure, the finale was the extraordinary,

choreographed routine of *Proud Mary*, but Tina was flaunting an image that was not unlike a Rock & Roll fusion of *Barbarella* and Brigitte Bardot, flanked by two statuesque dancers. The set list showed impeccable taste, including a stunning rendition of David Bowie's theme from *Cat People* and an all-out rock version of *Nightlife* by Foreigner. This was a credible set of songs, all given the Tina Turner treatment.

This concert was always on my mind and when I found myself in a position to book acts for *The Tube*, she was a recurring priority at planning meetings. Jools Holland and Paula Yates were big fans. In 1983 her British promoter, Barrie Marshall, informed me that he was bringing Tina Turner over and probably at considerable financial risk. When you book an act for television you enlist record company support for their act. If that act has a release out then they support it, if there is no release it is a different story. When I approached EMI over Tina Turner they were extremely reluctant and told me her re-signing to the label was in doubt as she was playing gigs like MacDonald's conventions (of course she was - she was supporting a family now she was out of Ike's clutches). The Ritz show that I had seen in 1981 was, in fact, an effort to showcase her talents for prospective managements.

Despite EMI's reluctance, Barrie Marshall shrewdly realised the career-defining potential for her in appearing on Friday night on the Rock & Roll circus that was *The Tube*. He reorganised her European tour and flew her from New Orleans to New York, London and Newcastle. I was at the airport when Tina Turner and her band walked off the plane along with The Eurythmics and Public Image Ltd!

Her performance on the show was even more exciting than the one I had seen at The Ritz. To give it even more credibility - and this was what the programme was very good at doing - we brought in two members of Heaven 17 as backing singers, who had showcased her on their remarkable BEF album. She also performed her version of Al Green's classic *Let's Stay Together*. which of course would chart. In the audience you can see Annie Lennox and Billy Bragg looking on. This appearance in November 1983 is seen now as the turning point in Tina Turner's career - it rebooted her into chart, touring, movie and stadium stardom.

A year later, EMI became obstructive when I requested an interview with Tina Turner during her recording of *We Don't Need Another Hero* at Mayfair studios in London. In the end I left a handwritten note of complaint to her manager at the Saint James' Club where I had earlier delivered her wig in a box directly from L.A. We did get the interview, but I was banned from EMI offices for going directly to the manager - in other words doing their job for them!

Perhaps *that* is why I am smiling in the photo.

duran duran *save a prayer*

I can only describe the photo opposite as *perspirational*. Behind me are Duran Duran rehearsing for the first international film shoot for *The Tube*.

I regard Duran Duran as superb pop craftsmen. They were a collision of dance sensibility, powerpop and New Romanticism. All this came packaged with incredible style, refracted through state of the art promotional videos which have never been surpassed. Most of the lineup hailed from Birmingham but the image that they created for themselves made them look more Sri Lanka than Selly Oak. They looked like the playboys of western pop, to a certain extent rebooting Glam.

I first met them when I was co-hosting *Look! Hear!* They made their world television debut in Studio 1 at Pebble Mill, performing *Planet Earth*. By the time I joined *The Tube* production team in 1982 they were one of the biggest bands on the planet. Because of my Birmingham connection with them it was felt that it would be a good diplomatic move to be a familiar face as they rehearsed a new album at a château near Nice. That is why I am standing, slightly dishevelled, as they tune their guitars. The half hour documentary *A Day With Duran Duran* was screened in 1983 to award-winning acclaim, it was directed by Geoff Wonfor who would go on to direct *The Beatles Anthology*.

Filming in the South of France was expensive so we spread the cost by snagging some interviews at Cannes Film Festival, scooping David Bowie. When in Cannes, I regularly passed a keyboard busker who I thought was rather good. It was actually Jean Michel Jarre, another busker turned out to be Wombles composer Mike Batt. This was all part of the Cannes film festival tradition.

chris phipps with members of duran duran, john and andy taylor.

david bowie *chaos in cannes*

In 1967, I knew Bowie's manager, Kenneth Pitt, quite well. At that time Bowie was attempting to emulate Anthony Newley by becoming an 'all-round' entertainer. He made a novelty record *The Laughing Gnome*, then became Ziggy Stardust, the androgynous visitor from another world, then soaked up electronic music, followed by soul music in America and then, in *Ashes to Ashes*, there was new wave romanticism! Incredible! He was a musical dilettante - the greatest shape-shifter in music. His work was also always visually inspiring and he was difficult to categorise as he had so many influences, making it difficult to identify the real him - but that's how he sold an album to No.1 with no pre-publicity! Keep 'em guessing!

When I was working on *The Tube* in 1983, David Bowie agreed to be interviewed by Jools Holland at Cannes Film Festival. Bowie was promoting his new film release *The Hunger*, a vampire film co-starring Catherine Deneuve, which was directed by North East film director, the late Tony Scott. He wanted to talk about his film, not his music. It was a huge coup to get him and, being an admirer of his talent, I will never forget the feeling when his PR found me to escort Jools and me to his room in a private apartment in Cannes. Wearing chinos and a simple shirt, he looked extremely relaxed and talked at length. He was the most charismatic person I have ever met. There was something very driven about him which appealed to people and certainly drew me to him. I felt very comfortable with him as he talked to me at length about his enthusiasm for making short films for the cinema. He thoroughly enjoyed being interviewed, talking about *Merry Christmas Mr. Lawrence*, *Just a Gigolo* and *The Hunger*. This was an intimate interview not a press circus.

I have always been fascinated by Bowie and I have rarely met anyone with such great presence.

ap

49

the tube *the weekend starts here*

The Tube launched on Channel 4 - not so much with a bang - but with a sparkler gripped by Jools Holland as the bemused audience filed up the tunnel entrance. A pregnant Paula Yates showed the delights of the cavernous Studio 5 and Sunderland's Toy Dolls blasted their way through a tribute to a Sunderland wine bar. The first show ended with The Jam's last ever gig - it inferred the end of an era and the promise of new one, filled with headline and unsigned acts and irreverent humour. By the end of the first series previously circumspect record companies were competing to get their act on and their A&R men watched avidly in London offices to spot raw talent showcased each week. I discovered a lot of that new talent - The Proclaimers, Fine Young Cannibals, Hollywood Beyond, Swansway and many others. At that time in Newcastle, the Live Theatre had found a home nearby but the Baltic Mill still made flour not modern art and the *Get Carter* car park still loomed over Gateshead. The gentrification of the Newcastle's Quayside was around the corner. At last, for five years Newcastle was Capital of Cool.

Many of you will recognise the actor standing between Jools Holland and myself (next page, top right) at the entrance to *The Tube* studio on City Road, Newcastle in the photo opposite. He is Peter Adamson, who for over twenty years portrayed Weatherfield builder and councillor Len Fairclough in *Coronation Street*. At the time of the photograph,

Adamson had been let go from the soap as a result of selling his story to the national papers. I was always keen on the idea of cross-referring names from other branches of entertainment onto the Friday night show. Adamson was an icon to television audiences, so to see him suddenly appear in the context of a rock show would be quite bizarre. At the time he was in a play in Guildford and I met him to broach the idea in a rather run-down lodging/guest house. We had quite a frank conversation and he seemed embittered. He told me that during his twenty-year tenure he had been afraid to commit to any outside publicity or appearances as Corrie stars were strictly controlled within the context of the production in its early years. He readily agreed to my proposal.

In his *Tube* appearance, he was seen working behind the bar, not of the Rover's Return, but of the Egypt Cottage pub on City Road, Newcastle. The pub was nicknamed Studio 6! As Jools introduces Paul Young, Adamson interrupts and, as he cleans a glass, announces a tirade of facts about Paul Young's history and influences, rather like a human wikipedia. It is comparable with the scene from *Wayne's World*, where Alice Cooper suddenly shows incredible expert knowledge on the Native Americans. As Peter Adamson still holds forth, Jools pulls a pump handle on the bar, resulting in Adamson falling into a pit of alligators. A rare moment that really worked. Peter really enjoyed his

rex

jools holland, peter adamson and chris phipps.

promotional pig over newcastle and the legendary tube entrance to studio 5.

time on the show and it is sad to know that he died a recluse in the 1990s.

My other attempts to cross-fertilise entertainments weren't so successful. When Derek was jilted at the altar by Mavis in Coronation Street, I wanted the actor who played Derek to sit at the bar looking dejected. He didn't even need to speak because everyone knew why he was there. His agent wasn't as keen as I was on the idea, so it didn't happen. On another occasion I wanted a Dalek to stand in the queue as the audience filed in to the entrance. The BBC wouldn't allow it as the Dalek could only be seen in the context of evil - how all this has changed with multi-media platforms for promotion.

I did succeed, and this is really bizarre, in getting Old Mother Riley (played by Steve King) to put in an appearance on the 1982 New Year's Eve show. Again, this nearly didn't happen because I was threatened with a law suit by someone else claiming to have inherited Old Mother Riley's likeness from originator Arthur Lucan. As they say, you couldn't make it up!

iggy pop the *return of the mummy*

The Albany Hotel is situated on Birmingham's Queensway. To me it always resembled a giant packet of John Player's Special cigarettes. In its shadow was Alex's pie stand. Here, late night Birmingham musicians would eat and drink and you would find Roy Wood, John Bonham and Tony Iommi engaged in conversation.

Here in the Albany restaurant sat Iggy Pop, whose lacerated upper torso was an iconic image of pre-punk hysteria as he fronted The Stooges in New York and crowd-surfed self-destructively over a sea of humanity. In this photograph he seems to be wearing some type of woad body paint and he had just come off stage at Birmingham Odeon where he had performed in support of one of his less successful albums on the Arista label. He looks distracted - and he was, mainly by fans waiting around the corner. He was also seizing pâté in a handful as the hors d' oeuvres trolley came by. For the only time in my career I knew that this interview would go absolutely nowhere and he knew it as well. We courteously agreed to part and it never happened.

Years later Iggy graced *The Tube* studio with his extraordinary torso. Two minutes before broadcast he was nowhere to be found and there was no way I could go on stage and sing *Raw Power*. My phone rang - it was reception. A hesitant voice on the other end said, 'There is somebody - or some*thing* - resembling a mummy wandering about in *The Tube* tunnel entrance.'

Mr Pop, head to foot in bandages, was then guided skilfully back on stage to perform.

iggy pop - 'what me?'

54

the *million dollar* quartet

My record-buying habits in the 1960s involved collecting EPs, usually four track, for 10/6 with covers of varying quality. The EP was a great way of getting a sample of the music you loved without having to fork out 37/6 for an LP. They had either four tracks from the LP or often two singles put together. The artists I always pursued for my collection were Little Richard, Fats Domino, Bo Diddley and Chuck Berry. Chuck and Bo were on the wonderfully colourful Pye 'R & B' imprint, a stunning combination of red and yellow centre label. Pye was a British company and licensed these recordings from Chess records in Chicago. Eventually Chess started to issue directly into the UK and I coveted the stark black centre label with its golden chess piece design. Chuck, Fats, Richard and Bo really were a billion-dollar quartet. Richard was often heard shrieking via the radio but Fats, Chuck and Bo came to us through cover versions by Buddy Holly, The Beatles and The Rolling Stones. In the USA many of the quartet's original compositions were sanitised and bleached by the likes of Pat Boone to cross them over to a white middle-class audience where Rock & Roll was perceived to lead to social threat through 'juvenile delinquency'. This billion-dollar quartet had such a history of mismanagement, racial discrimination and financial exploitation, it gave them individually fearsome pecuniary attitudes towards the business

- and some of it would confront me in later years.

In 2017, Chuck Berry died aged ninety. It was alleged that he always asked for a copy of the *Financial Times* to be in his dressing room and a cash advance would be pushed under the door prior to his live appearance. I found his live appearances unpredictable, as he normally sound checked during the first number with whatever band he picked up, but when he duck-walked you forgave him everything. There is an irony that the man who crystallised the teenage experience in two-minute masterpieces like *Sweet Little Sixteen* and *Johnny B. Goode* only ever achieved a number one in the UK with a pitiful music hall double-entendre *My Ding-a-Ling* - originally intended for, and wisely rejected by Fats Domino.

I often found myself having to deal with unrealistic financial demands from these artists. Fats Domino's attorney told me, 'Fats doesn't care about being on television, the only way that you'll get him interested is to offer him a Rolls Royce (a model that he doesn't already have) for his collection.' Needless to say, my budget at the time wouldn't cover a Mondeo, so it wasn't happening.

Bo Diddley, born Elias McDaniel, toured with his sister, The Duchess, on bass guitar, and a man called Jerome who played maracas. This hip-to-trip trio was immortalised by The Animals in *The Story of Bo Diddley*. The Bo Diddley 'sound', which he tore out of a rectangular guitar decorated with CND logos was a primeval shuffle most associated with the raw sound of songs like *Not Fade Away*. Bo, clad in a tartan jacket, would wham out waves of reverberation to create his trademark sound. It would seismically echo in the Kinks and The Who. Now you know why Eric Burdon often affected a tartan jacket on stage! I interviewed Bo Diddley in 1980 at Birmingham Locarno, where he was backed by a trio called the DBs. Sporting his signature sheriff's hat, he played a stunning set where some of the jokes were longer than the instrumentals. Backstage he told me that when he was walking the streets, out of work, Elvis Presley had stolen his 'wiggle' on stage! He said that Richard Berry, who wrote *Louie Louie*, wasn't even credited on his own song and fought for years to get his money prior to his death. Bo explained that to ensure his own copyright on his songs he often put his own name in the title - hence *Hey, Bo Diddley*, *Bo Meets the Monster* and *Bo Diddley is a Gunslinger*. He signed the original Pye EPs for me, then asked for photocopies so he could send them to his attorney for copyright investigation. Maybe he should have made a record 'Bo Diddley Was Ripped Off!' Fortunately, patronage by The Rolling Stones with support slots would create some form of pension for him, but he remained short changed. No wonder Prince would cry 'Slavery'.

chris phipps and little richard on city road, newcastle.

joe bangay

Little Richard? He had similar complaints about exploitation. He told me that when Pat Boone was charting with covers of his original songs, he was surviving as a dish washer in a diner in Macon, Georgia, the state that gave Little Richard Penniman his legendary moniker 'the Georgia Peach.' My route to working with Richard was circuitous. Little Richard was once described as 'looking like Tarzan and singing like Daffy Duck' which is pretty accurate. I had seen him touring with The Rolling Stones and The Everly Brothers, screaming his mini-masterpieces of sexual innuendo to the audience - *Good Golly Miss Moll* and *Tutti Frutti*, where the vocals were interspersed with a whoop effect that would be appropriated by Paul McCartney. On the package tours Richard was suited and booted with processed hair. As the 70s glammed up, his real roots (sexual and follicular, betraying his origins as a female impersonator) literally came out on stage. His hair was whipped into a confection and on stage at Wembley he sported a vest made of mirrors with the light exploding from him as he stood astride the piano. How do you get or book an act like this? As with Chuck Berry, there were rumours of a 'no pay, no play' policy surrounding him. He was also prone to religious fervour and, like the Reverend Al Green and Jerry Lee Lewis, viewed entertainment as a volatile source of sin. Remember, the devil is often said to have the best tunes, so Little Richard would go into the ministry, preach and relinquish the dark side.

My first attempt to book him for *The Tube* was to approach his legendary producer, Bumps Blackwell, who was alleged to have hammered nails into Richard's hands to make him scream while recording. Blackwell was also the first producer to recognise the talents of a young trumpeter called Quincy Jones. Bumps arrived at my hotel in L.A. with a guide as he had lost his sight. Hoping to book Richard for *The Tube* I had brought a show reel of selected performances including Pat Benatar. Bumps' guide spent most of his time describing the physical attributes of the female performers to his mentor. It was an honour to meet the man who masterminded the Speciality recordings of Richard and Sam Cooke, but even he couldn't pin down the unpredictable Little Richard who was finding a movie renaissance via the film *Down and Out in Beverley Hills*. In the search for Richard the action would eventually move to Edgware in London.

My salvation on the road to Richard came in the form of author Charles White, AKA 'Dr Rock'. A larger-than-life Irish chiropodist from Scarborough, Chas's eccentric passion for Rock & Roll in general and Little Richard in particular had earned him the unique position of being Little Richard's exclusive and uncompromising biographer. He tipped me off that Richard, whom he dubbed the 'Quasar of Rock', would be making a press call at London Hippodrome, emerging with a piano from the floodlit floor. I felt uneasy about the whole affair from beginning to end. But it was an introduction and it did promote Chas's book. Even Melvyn Bragg and Lord Sutch were mingling at the altar.

Then Chas came with better news. Little Richard

would grant an interview to promote his Warner Bros single from the movie *Down and Out In Beverly Hills*, which was reviving his credibility and ranking him with co-stars Nick Nolte and Bette Midler. The single was, in accordance with his religion, non-sacrilegious - it was *Great Gosh Almighty*. Richard would be available at the Edgware Road Piano Shop, and *The Tube's* Jools Holland would be the interviewer.

This sudden announcement actually precluded Jools conducting the interview as he wasn't available, so I (not reluctantly) stepped in.

I nervously plunged into the interview the following day as Richard sat at Elton John's piano, but being a consummate showman, he made me feel we had always known each other. My key question about the origin of his classic lyrics prompted him, to the shock of his management and Dr Rock, to actually speak the lyrics of *Good Golly Miss Molly!* - an iconic moment! I can never believe, even now, that I got to interview him - the man who put 'Awop bop a loo bop' into a million tattoos. He also revelled in the fact that Macca struggled in his Hamburg Beatle days to emulate the master's trademark whoops.

But Richard never did play *The Tube* - he played *Cannon and Ball's Casino* on ITV1 instead. We were stitched up proper!

I last saw him in 2003 outside the infamous Led Zeppelin 'Riot House', the Hiatt Hotel on Sunset in LA, sitting in a black stretch limo, attended by young flunkies like a modern Caesar, talking to the session players Pat and Lolly Vegas, the original founders of the Inuit band Redbone.

When Richard played Channel 4's *The White Room*, he made two demands. One - he must be announced as 'The Architect of Rock & Roll'. Two - cash, and lots of it, in the dressing room, brought in from the local bank. Who can argue? - Rock & Roll and Little Richard are a lethal cocktail.

chris phipps with little richard on the set of *the tube*, peter bensimon in the background.

ozzy osbourne let's go crazy

When Europe wanted theatrical rock imported from the USA we got Alice Cooper, Meat Loaf and, to a certain extent, Dee Snider and Marilyn Manson. We only needed to send one act back in exchange - the one and only Ozzy Osbourne. American culture gave us *The Wizard of Oz* we gave them the Blizzard of Oz. This photograph was taken at Castle Donington Monsters of Rock Festival in 1983. Five years before, in 1978, Ozzy had left/been fired from Black Sabbath. At the Birmingham Odeon I saw his final performance, spraying the front row with soda water, which promptly short circuited everything on stage. Van Halen were the support act. His first replacement was Dave Walker. Dave's only live appearance with them languishes in the archives of BBC Midlands TV - a performance of *War Pigs* on *Look! Hear!* The next time I met Ozzy was to promote his solo album *Blizzard of Oz*. The band included a phenomenal guitarist, the late Randy Rhoads. Ozzy was now managed by Sharon Arden, who would become his wife and, as one of the world's great managers, the reinventor of his career. Ozzy is the epitome of heavy metal theatricality. Heavy Metal as a genre contains elements of English entertainment, mediaeval mystery plays, Shakespeare, Hammer films, the Whitehall farce - all of them are there in Ozzy's stage persona. America first took to him as a rock version of *Barnum* (in a similar way the USA embraced Billy Idol as a UK token punk import).

In an even smarter move, Ozzy and family took over the reality TV screen as their daily arguments and goings on became part of the American zeitgeist. As Ozzy sang on one of Sabbath's few chart hits, *Never Say Die*.

The last time I met him was January 2017, when I worked on *Black Sabbath The End* movie. After I had conducted the interview at their palatial hotel near Dublin, an employee was heard to say on the phone that there seemed to be a Black Sabbath tribute act in reception but the Ozzy Osbourne didn't look convincing!

the very things *the bushes scream*

The Very Things hailed from my home patch of the Midlands, Redditch in Worcestershire to be precise. They were a trio consisting of Gordon Disneytime on drums, Robin Raymond on guitar and the formidable 'The Shend' on vocals. They are often described as being Dadaist Post Punk, whatever that is supposed to mean. The cassette which they sent me was intriguing. The Shend sounded like Nervous Norvus who had a cult hit with the sanguine song *Transfusion*. The Very Things created a cut up world of post punk, gothic images, the music hall and B-Movie science fiction. This is a mixture and approach to music I have always loved. We devised an epic promotional film for their track *The Bushes Scream While My Daddy Prunes*. In the film the enigmatic trio drive a television transmitter van into a cosy, suburban street. They park outside a house whose single unsuspecting occupant suddenly witnesses their performance which is beamed into his front room television set, interrupting normal transmission. The hapless viewer at the end of the performance is devoured by the plants in his own front garden à la *Day of the Triffids*.

The location of the suburban house was the Cowgate area of Newcastle. The house was owned by friends of the director Gavin Taylor. The unfortunate occupant was played by a local equity member and dance band member known as Billy. By the very nature of what was going on musically and plot-wise Billy's perplexed look in the video was genuine. Needless to say, occupants of the street were equally perplexed by the enigmatic transmitter van and plants moving around in the front garden. Maybe they thought they had been drinking the wrong kind of tea. The actual performance of the song itself was filmed in a chapel at Alnwick Castle. It took a lot of convincing to get the land agent for the castle to agree as they had been previously duped by soft porn film makers in a previous, unfortunate experience.

On the day of filming at Alnwick, ITV was hit by industrial action. The result was that every member of the crew had to be shadowed by their immediate boss. As a result there were so many people on location it looked as if we were filming the next James Bond epic.

The final result is one of the most original music films I have ever been involved with. It was shown on *The Tube*, amongst the wreckage of a midsummer special, also plagued by industrial action. The film today has a strong cult following. The Very Things would later appear live in the studio performing their classic track *Motor Town*, an amazing mixture of punk and Motown. The Shend also developed a successful career as a character actor on film and television. To me, the band are up there with outfits like The Residents, occupying a unique and enigmatic place in music.

chris phipps posing as salvador dali with 'the shend' and gavin taylor.

wrathchild stakk attak

Wrathchild were a Midlands Glam Metal band boasting a line-up that included names like Lance Rocket and Eddie Star. They were clad in Neo-BDSM outfits and had extraordinarily teased hairstyles and stack-heeled boots. They were signed to the appropriately titled Heavy Metal Records in Wolverhampton. Whatever the venue, Wrathchild put on an over-the-top Kiss-style show, so the grungiest pub audience still got bombarded with confetti and fireworks.

If they had been American, I think they would have received the backing and promotion accorded to Motley Crue who were not dissimilar. Left to their own resources in the Midlands, the band always made a valiant DIY approach to their art and gained a great deal of publicity. Like Kiss, what they might have lacked in musicianship they made up for in showmanship - which is why I wanted to capture them on film for *The Tube*.

We filmed Wrathchild on a freezing January day at the Black Country Living Museum in Dudley. The rusting machinery and forge hearths formed a sort of post-apocalyptic *Mad Max* scene. The band brought their biggest stage prop - a battle tank - that looked as though it had come from *Mad Max 2*. The band performed atop this huge contraption, whose guns fired confetti, accompanied by giant catherine wheels. The number they performed had the unsurprising title *Stakk Attak*. The sub-zero conditions worked in our favour. Director Geoff Wonfor was able to set up his camera on the roof of a narrowboat that was frozen in the middle of a canal, giving a superb wide view of the performance.

There is an interesting postscript. I received a call from DHSS, who had seen the performance on TV. They were trying to trace certain band members for benefit claims. Unfortunately for them, the only names I could give them were their stage names, as that was the only record I had. The woman from the DHSS was quite irate when I gave her a list of names that seemed to come from a graphic novel. I don't know whether her pursuit was successful.

wrathchild with director geoff wonfor (left).

no woman, no cry

I took the two photos on the far right in Government Yard in Trenchtown, Jamaica - this is the actual government yard - a ghetto community food facility - that Marley refers to in *No Woman No Cry* - a spiritual moment for any Marley fan like me. In Jamaica in 1983 I briefly encountered Bunny Wailer, who was knocking out the contents of a rather large pipe. I encountered the darker side of Jamaica as I was kidnapped at knifepoint when I was suspected of being CIA. *That* is another story…

Much of my time filming in Jamaica for Channel 4 was rather like being in a Jamaican version of *Twin Peaks*. It is a parallel universe. There pervades a sense of lawlessness and visions of poverty that you never quite assimilate. I was in pursuit of the legendary Gregory Isaacs, known as The Cool Ruler and singer of classics like *Night Nurse*. The problem was that he was on the run from the authorities, so he was afraid to turn up for filming most of the time. I managed to get him to sign a contract, surrounded by machete-carrying bodyguards, but we still didn't get to film him. More successful were lensing Sly and Robbie, the militant Black Uhuru and the wonderful Dennis Brown, who mimed his vocal walking along Hellshire Beach.

Jools Holland did an extraordinary interview with producer par excellence Lee Perry, who had produced amongst others Bob Marley and The Clash. Like many producers, Lee Perry was eccentric - in this case a pyromaniac. He had burnt down his Black Ark studios and Jools interviewed him outside the ruins. There were various items impaled on the gates including a toaster. He told Jools, 'It shows that I am a boaster, not a toaster.' The last time I met Lee Perry was in a council house in Enfield. Needless to say, half of it was burnt out.

Did I ever get to film Gregory Isaacs? Well, Island Records staged a reggae superjam for filming at Market Street Studios in London. It was a Who's Who of reggae - Steel Pulse, Aswad, Dennis Brown, Dean Fraser, Sly and Robbie and more jammed on Marley's *Get Up, Stand Up* but there was still no sign of Gregory. I found out where he was staying and where he was sleeping. His housekeeper warned me, 'If you go in there it will be like waking a sleeping lion.' I left the address of the studio and left. Eventually Gregory did turn up wearing a naval officer's uniform but unfortunately filming had finished.

Oh yes, I managed to meet King Tubby, the man who created Dub, in a ghostly suburb of Kingston. He was a shy, reticent man who came to an untimely end like many of Jamaica's creative community.

an frazer and dennis brown.

(Now) robbie shakespeare.

RIDDIM
TWINS
ICK HAARD
IDG
GREGG

madonna *one way ticket*

In the democracy of this book, arguably the biggest star gets the shortest story. In January 1984 *The Tube* decided to do an outside broadcast from the legendary Hacienda club in Manchester. There was a new act being promoted by Warner Brothers who I was told was a 'non- priority' strictly one-off act. She was called Madonna and she was promoting her slow burning eponymous album with performances of *Holiday* and *Burning Up*. She turned up in Manchester and dutifully performed. I was too preoccupied at the time to fully watch her lip-synch performance dancing with her brother Christopher. On that night she fitted the programme's eclectic bill perfectly, partly crossing over the New York gay club dance scene into Manchester's most notorious cool venue. Her appearance that night is now credited as helping to launch a phenomenon. Suddenly she *was* a priority act. This outside broadcast was under the production of myself and, a good friend and partner in musical crime, Mick Sawyer. Mick would eventually bring a great source of reggae and African music into *The Tube* mix.

Madonna's appearance, as with all acts, was governed by strict union rules. All acts were paid standard musician's union rates. This gave a financial equality to every performer whatever their status. Because she was American her backing track had to be re-recorded in England by British session musicians, not an easy call. Also, I had to exchange her British appearance for a reciprocal appearance by a British artist in America. It was not just a case of booking an act to walk on stage, it was an administrative maze. For some reason, Warner Brothers records had only paid Madonna's fare one way London to Manchester. Mick Sawyer and myself handed her a brown envelope containing £37 in cash for her return fare. The rest is history - but I don't think this is recorded in her autobiography…

It should be noted that Madonna's first British TV appearance was on the BBC's *Top Of The Pops* the night before *The Tube*.

alamy

rex

hollywood nights *in the hollywood hills*

Hollywood is a strange place. It exists only because of dreams - some of which come true, but the majority don't. As Burt Bacharach once wrote, most of the stars wind up pumping gas. If you are in music television it's Mecca. Thanks to *The Tube*'s worldwide music focus I was able to live the dream and actually visit buildings like the legendary Capitol Records Tower in Downtown Hollywood. *The Tube* filmed everything from The Red Hot Chilli Peppers playing on top of a giant hot dog to the Eurythmics launching their *Revenge* tour in The Valley Club.

I found Ex-Sex Pistol Steve Jones languishing in an apartment shared with a computer programmer. He had joined a band called Chequered Past whose line-up included members of Blondie and Tin Machine. They were fronted by Michael Des Barres, a Brit actor and singer. Despite one superb album, sounding like a cross between Def Leppard and The Sex Pistols, Chequered Past literally went there. We filmed Steve Jones in a short-lived line-up called The Dano Jones Band. The location was, in fact, more interesting. It was a gang-run breakers' yard where they built low riders. Needless to say, we filmed as quickly and politely as possible, but we were made very welcome. I felt sorry for Steve as he seemed stranded in the post-Pistols mess and we had interesting chats, particularly as former manager McLaren was at large in the same neighbourhood! That would have been an encounter to capture on film.

The Hollywood sign is an icon. It is said that the composer of *Nature Boy*, Eden Ahbez, who was the original hippy, lived under a letter 'L' and bummed doughnuts off passers-by on the strip. Pictured overleaf are Lone Justice performing to playback for *The Tube*. Their vocalist Maria McKee went on to world fame with the song *Show Me Heaven*.

On the next page (far right) is what I can only describe as an awkward moment framed by the Hollywood sign. The idea was for Malcolm MacLaren to interview Bryan Ferry. I am holding the sound boom for some reason. What seemed a good idea in the cold light of a Newcastle production office bombed completely in the heat of the Hollywood day. Malcolm MacLaren had his own agenda and there was just no chemistry between Bri and Malc. It wasn't that they disliked each other - it was just a forced chemistry that didn't work. Bryan Ferry was eventually interviewed by the director back at the hotel. We made a separate film with Malcolm MacLaren called *The Great Hollywood Swindle*, though it transpired that he couldn't fool the Hollywood studios in the way that he had manipulated the British record industry. He remains for me a fascinating and darkly hypnotic

ex-sex pistol, steve jones.

ferry, maclaren and phipps.

dangerous individual. He used to frequently say to me, 'If you are walking on eggs don't hop,' with a prankish look on his face.

David Coverdale, pictured below with bassist Neil Murray, was in a sort of musical exile living in a Hollywood hotel. Millions of dollars were being poured into recording what would be the album *1987*, which would become Whitesnake's calling card for world domination and blow-dried, wind-tunnel style promo videos. They had already had European success in the teeth of punk in the late seventies but this really was the crossroads for David's career. He told me that if this failed he would be a taxi driver as he had just passed his driving test in the USA. Needless to say, he didn't have to take that option. He remains a master showman, with an acute sense of loyalty to his fans.

I met up again with Bryan Ferry in 2001, interviewing him for the award-winning television series *Northstars*. Like many creative performers and composers, Bryan Ferry is a shy and reticent individual. When conducting an interview like this you need to find common ground right at the start to relax the situation so that they can open up without fear of me asking tabloid questions. We found we had a common love of Stax and Soul, in fact he has named his son Otis. From there it was cautiously plain sailing. I did pluck up the courage to ask him about the often-used description of Ferry as 'Sultan of Suave.' He replied that his teenage weekends spent window gazing in Marcus Price outfitters in Newcastle hadn't gone to waste.

david coverdale, chris phipps and neil murray, los angeles.

chris phipps with bryan ferry, le mondrian, 2002.

lone justice with maria mckee.

dire straits *brothers in arms*

In 1985 Dire Straits were the biggest band in the world. Led by charismatic guitarist, Mark Knopfler, they were the first pop/rock group to capitalise on the new compact disc format. Their album *Brothers in Arms* is the first original million-selling compact disc pop/rock recording. Their ordinary image makes their music even more extraordinary. Mark Knopfler, like many great musicians, was always reticent, making his statements through his music. Part of his muse came from his adoptive North East upbringing. One example, he told me about in an interview, was the song *Tunnel of Love*, a superb example of Straits' widescreen epic, yet intimate, sound. Audiences still think that the Spanish City referred to in *Tunnel of Love* could be Madrid or Barcelona. It is, in fact, the seaside amusement park on the coast at Whitley Bay in the north east of England, where a young Knopfler would escape, because he knew there he would find the blaring sound of Rock & Roll accompanying the rides. Over the years, he fused Celtic and other influences with Americana to create multi-platinum selling records. Mark Knopfler is a performer who never sought stardom or fame - he only ever wished to improve as a songwriter and guitarist. He has.

In the mid-1980s, the world tour in support of *Brothers in Arms* created such hysteria and picked up such momentum that it lasted almost three years. On *The Tube*, Phonogram records gave us access to filming the band in Jerusalem. As part of the documentary shoot, Paula Yates interviewed Mark Knopfler and relaxed with the band off stage. In the middle of filming in the centre of Jerusalem, the band decided to hire and ride donkeys. As you can see in one of the photographs, their manager, Ed Bicknell, looks slightly apprehensive. The scene turned out very well. However, when it was included in the finished film, I received an irate letter from the Animal Handlers' Association, saying that I should have cleared the ride with them before filming! How I was supposed to do this when it was a spontaneous decision by the band in the middle of Israel I do not know. Remember, at this time television was very strictly unionised, which had its advantages and its drawbacks. Another example from this shoot was that I handed Paula Yates an Israeli artefact and the scene was ultimately cut as I was not an authorised props handler.

The Dire Straits concert shoot was a quasi-military operation involving cameras on the ground and in the air. The band were performing in what was called The Sultan's Pool - a natural amphitheatre beneath the walls of Jerusalem. This venue had only played host to two pop acts before - Demis Roussos and Foreigner. No-one was prepared for the hysteria surrounding *Brothers in*

Arms. Security and policing were just not adequate and fans, most of them non-paying, were hurling themselves onto the stage from the rocks above. Fans were climbing and clinging to telephone poles and pylons within this natural arena. In unbelievable heat, it was a night of extraordinary tension, with the crowd threatening to storm the stage. Mark Knopfler, in his signature headband, soldiered through.

As with all foreign shoots, we had to deliver a documentary on the indigenous music scene to make the most of the budget. One act I discovered was an Armenian vocalist called Ofra Haza.

Armenian stars often performed on a circuit of garage cafes and her stunning vocals in *Im Nin Alu* brought her international stardom and sampling fame by such bands as Sisters of Mercy. She has passed into legend as part of the world music scene.

As a footnote, a Tel Aviv band gave me a promotional kit containing, as I discovered in Customs at Tel Aviv airport, a stolen army-issue bullet. As a result, I was questioned for quite a long time before being allowed to return home. The problem was compounded by the fact that I had been invited to guest on an army radio station during my stay!

above) dire straits and paula yates. *right*) ofra haza.

eurythmics *thorn in my side*

These are some of my favourite portraits in the book. They capture the charisma both of The Eurythmics' Dave Stewart and *The Tube's* Paula Yates. The location is the Mexican market area of Los Angeles. The occasion was a thirty minute feature on the launch of The Eurythmics 1986 album *Revenge*.

The live concert launch by the band was scheduled for The Valley Club in Downtown LA. Dave and Annie Lennox wanted different interview locations to talk about the album. Both would be interviewed by Paula Yates and her husband, Bob Geldof ,would introduce the band on stage - he had just been knighted.

Annie Lennox's team said that the interview with her would be 'a stream of consciousness!' I told them that *The Tube* didn't have too many James Joyce readers amongst its viewership. They climbed down and the interview was conducted in an open top American car on the move with a police escort as we filmed. Dave Stewart did a more conventional walk and talk with Paula through the Mexican market area - every stall holder who came in vision had to be paid - an expensive walk! I booked a Mariachi band via a donut stall which doubled as an agency.

The live set later that day was a stormer, the new band included Blondie drummer Clem Burke. Dave and Annie affected a stunning black leather and white shirt combo look. They have always been masters of image.

One footnote: because of the time delay between LA and Newcastle, insurance only came through for the entire gig, by fax, fifteen minutes before they broke into *Thorn In My Side*. In addition, director Geoff Wonfor went down with a raging tooth abscess, so I had to take him to a local hospital. Whatever they shot into him worked!

aula yates and dave stewart, los angeles, 1986.

livin' *in the 80s*

Pictured (next page, bottom) are Killing Joke fronted by the charismatic and scary Jaz Coleman. This band (and this is why I like them) defy any category. Critics have dubbed them proto-industrial, gothic and prophets of doom and gloom. They were a huge influence on bands like Metallica and Nine Inch Nails. The occasion is their appearance on *The Tube* and they are a fine illustration of the methods I had to employ scouting for and booking acts for the show. This particular method is called 'going to a festival!' - a good way to catch the music zeitgeist. I first saw Killing Joke at the extraordinary Futurama Festival, which was a Punk/New Wave gathering at what had been a tram shed in central Leeds. Most of the audience seemed to be sleeping in cellophane on the floor and eating meat pies. I saw Killing Joke and booked them on the spot. I knew they were right for Channel 4's cutting edge music show. They fitted perfectly into the organised chaos of Studio 5. Top right in the photograph is the late Paul Raven. I had booked Paul years before when he was a member of

Neon Hearts in Wolverhampton for a BBC drama directed by Philip Saville. Paul's passing in Switzerland was a sad loss.

Another act I booked from Futurama was Billy Bragg, whose defiant rendition of New England won me over. Billy comes from a long line of broadside singers and activists like Ewan MacColl. In the photograph (next page, top) he is engaged in conversation with Bono backstage. Maybe they were planning to form a new band. Billy has recently written a very fine history of skiffle music.

The third act I found at Futurama was Southern Death Cult, fronted by Ian Astbury. They shortened their name to The Cult the night they played *The Tube*. I always considered that after that they had a bad attack of 'Led Zeppelin'. Wasn't Billy Duffy in The Smiths? The most extraordinary memory of Futurama was the Sunday headline act The Bay City Rollers. There they were, Woody and the boys, their original ageing fans waving scarves, sandwiched between a sea of punks and the stage. *Bang Shang A Lang* indeed.

top) billy bragg and bono at studio 5.
right) killing joke with chris phipps (RIP paul raven, top right).

run dmc! *walk this way*

Walk This Way by Run DMC and Aerosmith is a milestone. It was the first time these two opposing styles of music - Rock and Hip Hop - had mixed, with explosive results, an ultimate crossover cultural statement.

The problem is that the first promo video of *Walk This Way* completely failed to register this unique mix. This is how it happened. When a promotional video is made the producer is supplied with a cassette and then a playback tape of the track to be filmed. This essentially means that all artistes mime their performance to a backing tape so that the director and crew can cover each mimed performance from a different angle. These are then edited together to achieve the final product, which hopefully will result in the record going into the charts by a television promotion on the likes of MTV. Using live vocals would be expensive and unpredictable.

I was given the promotional cassette and backing track for *Walk This Way* when I was filming in Los Angeles in 1986. I was stunned by the track and, despite my comments and enquiries, was *never* told that Aerosmith were involved. I was convinced that what was actually Steve Tyler's vocal refrain and Joe Perry's guitar work were actually voiced by the Run DMC trio with a fantastic session band.

Oblivious to the facts, I proceeded to arrange a video shoot in Los Angeles, knowing that we didn't have Run DMC for very long. On Sunset Strip I found a collection of classic American cars that would form a perfect background. They were housed in the underground car park of a condominium. The crew set up and, as for any playback mime session, the backing track of *Walk This Way* was played through a big portable PA system. Run DMC arrived, clearly under pressure for time, and were distracted by the car collection. To the concern of the owner, the trio proceeded to jump impatiently in and out of some of these priceless cars. Fortunately, we got under way and the track was covered in about an hour. The band mimed Tyler's vocals as well as their own. The final promotional video was screened on *The Tube*, still with no reference to Aerosmith whatsoever. You can imagine the surprise on my face when I saw the American promo on MTV, complete with Aerosmith breaking through the brick wall of the apartment.

run dmc - 'where's
aerosmith?'

alamy

miles davis *running the voodoo down*

Miles Davis was once asked what he did for a living. His reply was that he had re-written musical history at least three times - and he was right. Here was a man whose trumpet playing was of such intensity and purity he could have contentedly rested on his laurels for a lifetime as an iconic player of Bebop and cool jazz. Yet the mercurial Miles Davis wasn't satisfied with this and he pushed the boundaries and the envelope of the jazz form beyond its limits. In 1970, his album *Bitches' Brew* emerged with extraordinary artwork and an even more extraordinary sound. Miles assembled a bewildering array of talent in the studio including guitarist John McLaughlin, who grew up in Monkseaton in the north east of England. The album was a malevolent, challenging reinterpretation of Miles' jazz heritage and virtuosity. By the time I saw him play at Ronnie Scott's club, his band were playing cross-over rock venues in Europe and America. He had forsaken urbane threads for psychedelic colours and outsize shades. Playing with his back to the audience, he was a sorcerer's apprentice stirring up a soup of electricity and pulsating rhythm.

Later in his career he took on the appearance of The Mekon from Dan Dare and with his rasping voice he had a formidable reputation. Unbelievably, he turned up with his manager to be interviewed on *The Tube*. Jools Holland, with some apprehension, did a great interview, though Miles seemed more interested in sketching while he was answering. I rarely collect autographs but this is one I had to have. I proffered Miles the frontispiece of his biography written by Ian Carr. Miles hesitated with his pen and I suddenly thought 'what if he doesn't *approve* of this biography?' He did sign it and do a quick sketch for me of a heart, which I treasure to this day. After the interview Miles retired to The Rose and Crown pub on City Road with his trumpet. The publican Jimmy Butterfield, a man not known for diplomacy, told him that he was 'not allowed to play *that* in here', refering to the most famous trumpet in the world, in the confines of the pub. Miles reaction is not recorded!

'The only colour I see is in my music' Miles Davis RIP.

bangay

To my knowledge, this is the only time Joan Armatrading and Elton John have performed together and they are performing in a barn for a reasons that will become clear. In 1987 I was commissioned to produce a documentary series for Channel 4 entitled *Acoustic*. It was an attempt to emulate MTV's *Unplugged* series. Performers would have a choice of guests and perform in a no-frills, stripped-back situation. The subject of the first *Acoustic* was Joan Armatrading, who was conveniently launching her first self-produced album *The Shouting Stage*.

Joan, who got her first guitar in Birmingham when her mother obtained it in exchange for an old pram, was a consummate performer, songwriter and guitarist. Like many perfectionists, Joan was intensely private, but she was happy to be interviewed for the one-hour documentary by the great Paul Gambaccini. I was elated by her possible choice of guests. She told me she was a big fan of both Mark Knopfler and Jimmy Page, but neither was available. There were still some great alternatives. From America, we flew in Bobby McFerrin, who had had a world number one with *Don't Worry, Be Happy*. Joan admired his incredible musicality. I had previously filmed him in L.A. performing a song where he used the resonance of his chest and limbs to accompany himself on vocals. In addition to McFerrin, Joan admired Elton John, who she felt could add his unique vocals to a song called *Stronger Love*.

Involving a star of the magnitude of Elton John is not easy. It is rather like playing a pin table - you need to know the nudges and the systems to apply to reach a goal. I am not giving away any trade secrets, but Elton got to hear of Joan's request. We were filming the interviews and performances at a livery stable business that she ran and a barn had become a makeshift studio. At the appointed time, Elton arrived in a burgundy-coloured limousine. I was so nervous that for some reason I called him Paul at least twice, which he found highly amusing. He stayed with us the whole day and the duet was wonderful. Under musicians union regulations I had to offer him a cash session fee. This he politely had sent to the charity London Lighthouse. He told me the last time he was offered cash was for playing a session for The Barron Knights!

At Olympic Studios, Joan wanted to replace a guitar break that she had been unhappy with during filming. She walked in and replaced it in one take, with the same seamlessness that she had displayed when I first saw her supporting Supertramp at Birmingham Odeon. The space and economy of *Love and Affection* dazzle me to this day

The *Acoustic* programme was greeted with indifference and, due to a change in commissioning editor at Channel 4, never got past the Joan Armatrading edition. The bitter irony is that the next programme would have been Roy Orbison, whose wife had agreed to the deal. Sadly, it would have been his epitaph.

Elton John and Joan Armatrading duet on *stronger love*, 1987.

black sabbath *forged in brum*

Black Sabbath was the collective sound of Tony Iommi, Geezer Butler, Bill Ward and vocalist Ozzy Osbourne. In the late 1960s they transcended the British Blues boom to create their signature mix of doom-laden riffs and imagery that the world would come to know as heavy metal. Maligned and often misinterpreted, Sabbath's sound would be vindicated by generations of younger musicians and the world success of the band's own reunion album entitled appropriately *13*. Although they are labelled as the originators of heavy metal, which itself is a proto-industrial sound, I have always felt that the band also had a punk ethic in their relentless 'do-it-yourself' approach to the sound they originated. They were punks before punk was even invented. They are, of course, equally infamous for their line-up changes and internal battles, mainly revolving around Messrs. Osbourne and Iommi.

This 1992 photograph (next page, bottom) was taken for a series I produced for Central and Channel 4 entitled *Motor City Music Years*, a personal history of Midlands' pop and rock. We are all looking very pleased with ourselves as we stand in front of a private chapel in the grounds of a Warwickshire ladies' finishing school. I chose the location because it was near their homes. The headteacher of the school constantly asked me what sort of music these musicians made. I euphemistically told her it was neo-classical - along the lines of Wagner. Thankfully she didn't come and check. For me Wagner is the father of heavy metal anyway.

In 2017 I had the honour of interviewing the final reunion line-up minus Bill Ward for director Dick Carruthers' documentary movie *The End*. It was extremely moving to see Sabbath performing for a multi-generational crowd of fans with an intensity and dedication that has endured five decades of falling out, legal wrangles, and, recently, life threatening illness. A tough act to follow - forged in Birmingham.

miriam phipps bertram

top) tony iomii and chris phipps at the
whitley bay film festival, 2018.
right) chris phipps with sabbath's
geezer butler and tony iomii, 1991.

the dales diary

The Dales Diary transmitted to an army of devoted viewers in the ITV Tyne Tees /Yorkshire Television region, opening its pages in 1991. For two months of every year it epitomised the best of regional television, portraying the Dales' life in a gentle but insightful way in magazine format. Some have compared it to a television version of *The Dalesman* magazine.

The Dales Diary profiled farmers, entrepreneurs, artisans, craftspeople, local historians, artists, writers and many other individuals whose lives and enterprise contributed to the regional and cultural identity of the programme's title. Here you would find real Dales' folk, no local soap stars or ghost hunters! For most 'Diary' guests it was probably their only experience in front of the camera. Key to this was presenter Luke Casey. He was synonymous with the series, striding the Dales every week with his signature walking stick. He seemed to walk eternally from one encounter to another. Luke had the provenance of being a formidable journalist and former co-presenter of BBC television's *Nationwide* magazine. He would put a guest at ease in front of the film crew in locations ranging from deserted moorland to bustling villages.

From 1992 I had the production task of scouting for programme subjects. My search for natural characters took me from Teesdale to Calderdale and Lancashire to the Whitby coast and all points in between. My discoveries were memorable. There was Arthur Mann, a Dales' piano tuner. We filmed him in his juddering Reliant three-wheeled van as he took to the motorway on his next job. It was like a cross between *Monty Python* and *The Fast and the Furious*. Eventually Arthur made it to Snape Castle to tune the chapel harmonium. Still on the move there was veteran cyclist 'Gig' Lee, who defied a leaking heart valve and doctor's orders to recapture his cycling touring days in Coverdale. With a storm behind him, he came flying over the hill through scattering sheep and luckily his heart and his tyre valves held out! Who can forget Angela Eddon who made besom brooms on the North York Moors? We filmed the North York Moors train actually stopping to take the brooms on board, on their way to sell at swanky Harrods in London. Of course once the series was established people would recommend subjects who would live just over the hill or round the corner. They ranged from a bovine chiropodist to an organ builder, a mole catcher, even a Spanish dry stone waller. We seemed to film at the top - the challenges of living at Dent Station and The Tan Hill Inn - to literally plumbing the depths where we found ourselves precariously at the bottom of Gaping Gill.

The Dales Diary uncovered local contributors.

Keighley historian Ian Dewhirst MBE guided Luke in the footsteps of J.B. Priestley and along the Bronte Way which had just been completed. Culinary historian Peter Brears found us regularly in the heritage kitchen at Hutton-le-Hole Museum. Here, he would conjure up historic dishes, including the medieval ancestor of Yorkshire parkin, an early form of digestif.

The series never failed to deliver over seventeen years, despite hazardous locations, torrential floods and a lethal foot and mouth disease outbreak.

The Dales Diary closed its pages in 2008 when ITV ceased regional programming and that vital local identity was eroded. *The Dales* was a later ITV network series fronted by Ade Edmondson which aimed to recapture some of *The Dales Diary* spirit. Even today people still ask me with affection whether *The Dales Diary* will ever re-open, because they can't quite believe that the programme's warm familiarity has gone from the screen and they can no longer make 'an appointment to view'.

(*The Dales Diary* was a ITV Tyne Tees/Yorkshire Television co-production with Zenith North/Zenith Entertainment/Peter Mitchell Productions 1991-2008.)

above) chris phipps and luke casey on location at holy wells.
right) at aysgarth with steve falvey on camera.

the paradise club
brothers with armaments

Zenith Entertainment produced films and television with worldwide success. Their movies launched the careers of everyone from Gary Oldman to Denzel Washington. They were big players in television drama. *The Paradise Club* was a drama series which would launch actor Lesley Grantham on his post-*Eastenders* career. I always find it ironic that the BBC had banned a record by Whisky and Sofa entitled *Dirty Den*. I think the grounds for banning it were for tastelessness or offence.

Lesley Grantham was paired with uber character actor Don Henderson. They played East End brothers. Grantham, you guessed it, played a loveable wide-boy/gangster whilst Henderson, as his brother, was a priest. Their collective scrapes, arguments and fortunes were set against a supposed dodgy music and drinking venue called The Paradise Club.

Because of the nature of the plot a lot of music was going to be needed, supervised by one of the best in the business - Graham Walker. The original plan was to 'manufacture' acts from equity members and film them performing as the script required. I was in and around Zenith producing Joan Armatrading and Walker sounded me out as to the types of music they might need for a 90s' club. I

told him and producer Selwyn Roberts not to fake the atmosphere with manufactured acts - it would look forced. I was given carte blanche to run 'The Paradise Club' like a real club and bring in unsigned acts so that it would offer an unusual showcase for them. Once the word was out audition tapes turned up by the sackful and we filmed a wide variety of performers. One of the best was a Dublin act called The Best Way to Walk but, like the rest of those who appeared, being on the television didn't ensure success and in retrospect sent a mixed message.

There was one exception. One script called for a competition featuring 'Britain's worst band' performing *Gimme Some Lovin'*. On stage the band were clearly wearing fright wigs and at a given moment they threw them off. The band were revealed to be Bruce Dickinson and Nicko McBrain from Iron Maiden, actor/bassist John Altman AKA Nick Cotton and Culture Club harmonica player Judd Lander. The audience at home couldn't quite believe what they had seen. Maiden's front man, the true Renaissance man that is Bruce Dickinson went on to appear as an AWOL rock star in a future episode. Another guest spot went to British crooner Denis Lotis - as urbane as ever.

The Paradise Club, despite two series, never really ignited. One problem was that the BBC put it up

'den' and don.

against the Michael Elphick programme *Boon*, which had a huge loyal following. The BBC letter of decommission actually arrived by second class post.

The series was initially filmed at Brixton Academy where security informed the producer that there was a 'dodgy looking bloke' on the premises - it was me, not Lesley Grantham. The location then moved to Camden Palace where you couldn't discern between real and fictional gangsters. In fact the legendary Dave Courtney was on security.

Selwyn Roberts and Graham Walker always gave me complete creative freedom on their projects which is a rare thing. I was later involved through them in booking acts for a Channel 4 drama *Comics* and a movie that required a Beach Boys tribute band. This would have been an act called Gidea Park but the music budget was scrapped when rain ruined the main outdoor sequences and had to be replaced by CGI. I also scouted rock act Reef for a movie, again set in the East End, about bare knuckle fighting, featuring Tim Curry. This again never got past the scouting stage and the movie was never made. That's show business!

brian wilson *love and mercy*

This is one of the few occasions I have been in the presence of a true musical genius. The year was 1988 and the place was Ku Club in Ibiza. There is quite a backstory to this photograph. Wilson was accompanied by his controversial manager and mentor Dr Eugene Landy whose relationship with Wilson has always sparked heated debate. The occasion of the photograph was a television spectacular entitled *Ibiza 92*.

The previous year, following the demise of *The Tube,* I was contacted by its director Gavin Taylor who was one of the world's 'go-to' directors for live concert movies and television. He told me he had become involved with Fugitive Television whose owners were producing *The Krays* movie. They also had responsibility for an annual entertainment event entitled *Ibiza 92*. This would run for five years up to the Barcelona Olympics in 1992, culminating in a massive televised concert. I was brought in to book 1987, 1988 and 1989 and it was no easy task. The first show in 1987 was a no-brainer. A six act bill was topped by the wondrous pairing of Freddy Mercury and Montserrat Caballet, performing the anthemic *Barcelona*. This was one of the first events to cross opera into pop. These were the best two artistes for the task, backed by full orchestra and choir. The location was the lofty Ku Club, a maze of swimming pools and dance areas, all rather decadent. The support bill included Marillion, Spandau Ballet and Duran Duran whose stock may have been low in Britain but was still very popular in certain European territories.

The following years' events, following the success of 1987, became over-ambitious and were complicated by the involvement of MTV. The trick is to book acts that appeal to all territories worldwide because an act that is big in Spain may mean nothing in America. The line-ups therefore became very bewildering, trying to please too many people in too many places all of the time. Brian Wilson shared a bill that included Tom Tom Club and Steve Earle. The gig was chaotic and another performer - the wonderful Nona Hendryx (ex-Labelle) cut her head on an underwater camera when she spontaneously dived into the swimming pool during her performance. Brian Wilson performed *Love and Mercy* but was under such pressure that he had to start the number at least six times. In the end of course he delivered as only he could.

Over the years *Ibiza 92* featured everybody from The Wonderstuff, Siouxsie and the Banshees, Prefab Sprout, Poison, Belinda Carlisle, The Moody Blues and prior to their fall from grace - Milli Vanilli. I always remember their contract stipulated the colour of cars to be provided and where models, hired for the occasion, should stand!

I even found myself doubling as an MTV interviewer to talk to Natalie Cole and Robert Palmer. I also turned around on one occasion and there was the one and only Frank Zappa who I think was just passing through. Inevitably there was panic in some quarters as the bill expanded and one promoter involved told me I would go to prison for booking too many acts.

The final event in '92 in Barcelona again featured Freddy and Montserrat performing their duet. As with any television event of this magnitude artists mimed to playback. The problem was as Freddy and Montserrat warbled away the playback tape ran a fraction under. This caused incredible editing problems for Gavin Taylor who had to re-sync the whole recorded performance second by second. Also on the bill was Rudolph Nureyev. He had an entire score faxed from Los Angeles and then decided *not* to go with it. His appearance on stage in a straw boater hat and striped swimming costume caused to, say the least, mixed reaction. The title of the event appropriately in Spanish was *La Nit*. As a footnote, many artists suffered in translation in the souvenir programme. For some reason Duran Duran were described as 'known for their sound and their famous two ton truck'.

They weren't too pleased as I passed them to board Queen's private jet on Barcelona runway.

with brian wilson, ibiza, 1988.

single *luck*

In the mid-90s I found myself producing for the Amsterdam based company IDTV. They produced a very successful series called *Single Luck*, which so far has only ever been shown on the continent. The idea of the series, rather like *Classic Albums*, was to profile in detail the composition, production and chart impact of Dutch chart 'one hit wonders.' Series one had concentrated exclusively on Dutch language artistes like The Dolly Dots, but now they wanted to expand their horizon to British and American stars, so I was brought in to locate them. This was quite challenging, as many acts had disbanded or just didn't want to talk about it. Some regard the expression 'one hit wonder' as a shameful curse, others see it as a financial and creative blessing. To have a 'one hit wonder' across many territories can give you a lucrative income for life - after all you only need one hit.

Some of these hits would be classed as flukes or novelties. A good example, which I refused to include was Rick Dees' *Disco Duck*. For others, particularly for seasoned musicians, it can be the one time that the stars align for your place in recording history. Carl Douglas told me that he only had to take one of his gold discs for *Kung Fu Fighting* into the bank and it would guarantee him a loan. He was a wonderful man, whose observation of kids playing Kung Fu pin tables in Soho inspired

his legendary hit. In Connecticut I interviewed Bobby Hebb, whose original version of *Sunny* was actually in the charts simultaneously with Georgie Fame's version. So grateful was Bobby Hebb for the success of this song world-wide, particularly with cover versions such as that by Cher, that he eventually became a voluntary highways' supervisor so that he could give something back to the community that had bought his record.

In Pittsburg we met and interviewed The Marcels, whose frantic vocalese version of *Blue Moon* is one of the pinnacles of doo wop music. It had been recorded in a snowbound New York studio as a one-take filler. It was produced by Stu Phillips, who would go on to compose the themes of *Knight Rider* and *Battlestar Galactica*. For all the worldwide success of that record, I found that the surviving Marcels were not living in the domestic or financial style that they should have been. They were quite difficult to track down, but it took one phone call after a search through the Pittsburgh phone directory to happen upon the cousin of the original lead singer. They shared the unusual surname of Harp, so there weren't many in the phone book.

Pictured are two acts closer to home. The first picture (next page) is of members of Unit Four Plus Two reunited in their local pub to perform the

unit 4+2 reunited with chris phipps.

wonderful *Concrete and Clay*. It is said that the tune inspired *It's Not Unusual* recorded by Tom Jones. Unit Four grew out of the London/St. Albans glee club and beat group scene. Their drummer, Bob Henrit, went on to The Kinks and Argent and the Spanish guitar in the song was played by Russ Ballard, who went on to back Adam Faith and write hits for Hot Chocolate and Rainbow among many. He proved too elusive to interview.

The second picture is of Peter Sarstedt (next page). Peter was a bon viveur and the success of his whimsical sardonic composition *Where Do You Go To My Lovely?* seemed to be more of a burden than a pleasure. Despite having his own television series off the back of the hit, he didn't really like the limelight or the spotlight - gigging only when he felt like it.

I went with him to Copenhagen, carrying his original handwritten lyrics for *Where Do You Go To My Lovely?* He wrote this when he was being hidden by his future wife in the attic of the nurse's home where she worked in Copenhagen. The attic - and the stove - were still there and he sat there recalling how the lyrics came to him in a dreamlike state. It was quite magical to recall and restage this candid moment and capture it on film. He also told me that the accordion break was recorded by a busker that the producer found in Leicester Square, who vanished into the streets after recording at Lansdowne Studios.

'One hit wonders' are rife with irony. Jeff Christie from Leeds wrote a song called *Yellow River*, which he offered to The Tremeloes. They recorded it then decided not to release it, so Jeff substituted his vocals on the track. *Yellow River* went on to sell millions and would have prolonged The Tremeloes' faltering career, though they did have a Spanish language hit version of it in South America. That's the way the cards fall.

Finally, a wacky moment with the diminutive Lynsey de Paul. (next page, bottom) Lynsey was rather like the princess in the tower. Romantically linked with James Coburn, she lived alone in a gothic house in Hampstead. She and Coburn had become interested in Oriental gong therapy. She insisted on demonstrating this for me by placing a copper bowl on my head and hitting it. If going slightly deaf is therapy, then it worked.

top) peter sarstedt, copenhagen, 1996.
right) bowled out by lynsey de paul.

ub40 *promises and lies*

I have always admired Birmingham band UB40 for their superb quality control and selection of the songs that they have covered - they have shrewdly remained outsiders, controlling their trajectory over the years as the world's biggest selling popular reggae band. The photograph shows them on location at a power station in Leicester filming a promotional film for a track on their album *Promises and Lies*. Each track was filmed by a different director including one by actor Keith Allen who posed as a taxi driver boasting to his passengers about his exclusive access to his mates UB40. This multimedia approach to marketing the album was the brainchild of UB40 saxophonist Brian Travers who is an extremely talented director - and a great guy.

Brian asked me to write a screenplay for a corporate promotional film to launch a new computerised stage lamp. I had just seen James Cameron's movie *The Abyss* and I had a bad attack of inspiration. In my story the lamp is the only source of light in a world of darkness deep underground in a vast tomb. It is discovered by a 'Luminaut' searching for new light. Under Brian's direction and a very resourceful team the product looked fantastic. The underground tomb set was in fact the deserted cellars of the old Bird's Custard Factory near their DEP studios.

A year later I met a technician who had seen the film at an American trade fair. He didn't know I had written it. He said to me, 'I saw this film which looked like *Alien*,' but I just couldn't understand what it was about - I don't think James Cameron lost any sleep. Brian still tours with UB40 and owns a successful art gallery in Birmingham.

The photograph (next page, top) shows left to right Chris Phipps, Brian Travers and producer Rupert Style on set.

filming in a power station, leicester.

© Richard Whitehead (www.richwhitehead.com)

john barry *mercury rising*

John Barry died in America, far from York where he was born in 1933. John was the son of a Yorkshire cinema owner and a concert pianist. This combination was destined to shape a career that would earn him five Academy Awards, four Grammys and countless honours at home and abroad.

There are few cinema goers untouched by his compositions. From the glitzy swagger of *James Bond* to the epic sweep of *Dances with Wolves* or *Born Free*, there is something for everyone, including me.

As a Northern-based film maker and producer I always hoped that our paths would cross. In this business, to quote James Bond, you never say never.

As producer of the Yorkshire/Tyne Tees television series, *Dales Diary*, I interviewed Pickering resident Keith Snowden. Keith had made a valiant attempt to turn Pickering into Hollywood with his locally made films. He had managed Pickering Cinema for Barry's father, Jack Prendergast, and recalled that young John was a proficient projectionist by the age of fourteen. More significantly, John would practise his trumpet skills in the conveniently empty auditorium. This was the very beginning of the John Barry Seven, who would headline at the family's Rialto cinema in York. John was a reluctant frontman but it was a shrewd way of getting into the emerging 50s' scene of British Rock & Roll. Another *Dales Diary* encounter was with an ex-John Barry Seven member at Aysgarth Carriage Collection. He told me that the group's exit from Yorkshire to London in 1957 would ignite John Barry's entry into arranging and composing for pop star Adam Faith. The rest would be movie history.

In 1998, Yorkshire Television asked me to produce a series entitled *Masterclass*. As the title suggests, students of everything ranging from fashion design to acting would receive a masterclass from their particular idol. John Barry was the obvious choice for film composing. Somehow, I obtained his home number in America and nervously put the idea directly to him. The voice at the other end of the transatlantic line was a mixture of broad Yorkshire vowels and Stateside twang. 'I love the idea,' he told me, 'But I'm scoring a Bruce Willis movie. Can you bring the student to me at my home?'

All things come to he who waits. Suddenly I was arriving at his Oyster Bay home next to Billy Joel's house. There was John Barry, frail, standing on a jetty with mist receding from the water, not unlike a scene from *The Lion in Winter*, which had won him an Oscar.

He showed me his collection of gold statuettes, which were overshadowed by an enormous portrait of a Yorkshire pig, hung over the New England fireplace. He recalled growing up in York and family outings to the moors and Dales. A regular family treat was York ham and eggs for tea at an old mill house. His young eyes would look at York Minster across the vale. Here he learned composition and arrangement for piano, the wartime deaths of his school staff would profoundly influence the tragic elements of his scoring. There was humour too - when he was approached to compose *Out of Africa*. The producer filled the office with copies of *Zulu*, a previous Barry work. John had to point out tactfully that there was no similarity.

As a film composer you are first over the top of the trench, it is an incredible responsibility because it is your job to tell a paying audience what to expect for the next two hours.

I last saw John at the Royal Albert hall conducting *You Only Live Twice*. Then he was gone.

His last solo project shows him standing on the limestone pavements of Ingleborough. It is wonderful to think that John Barry's moorland and dales upbringing found its way forever into the epic sweep of music for the American plains and African Transvaal.

john '007' barry with chris phipps, new york, 1998.

graham fellows *dumped!*

As booker and producer on *The Tube*, I received audition tapes by the ton. They regularly included recordings by a redundant security man by the name of John Shuttleworth. John clearly had a Bontempi organ in his front room and sang songs about domestic arguments with his wife Mary over the use of a vacuum cleaner. I always felt a mixture of pity and amusement at John's predicament and brand of entertainment. He had me fooled. In 1987, a music publisher who had a photograph of John in his office revealed to me that John Shuttleworth was the alter-ego of actor and musician Graham Fellows. Fellows had in fact had a previous incarnation as the punk saddo 'Jilted John' who topped the charts with *Gordon is a Moron.*

The portrayal of John Shuttleworth is a very fine piece of comedic acting, as opposed to being a comedy act. Graham creates a virtual world inhabited by John, his wife Mary, his next door neighbour and manager Ken and other characters such as dinner lady Joan Chitty. Over the years John's exploits have enthralled radio listeners and theatre audiences alike.

I was intrigued by the television potential of the character. Fellows' publishers financed a low budget pilot called *John Shuttleworth's Guide to Stardom*. We created John's front room world at a house in Wembley into which stepped Gary Christian, Mari Wilson and Beaky from sixties popsters Dave Dee, Dozy, Beaky, Mick and Titch! To John's chagrin he turned out not to be the real Beaky but a man who had leased the real Beaky's likeness! *The Guide to Stardom* was viewed by Granada and the BBC, but was never commissioned, they went for *Mrs Merton* instead. It was a learning curve for me as producer to work for a volatile talent. The director was Michael J. Wadding from Teesside.

In retrospect, Graham Fellows was probably done a favour by the non-commission. Apart from two feature films he has resisted the temptation to turn Shuttleworth into a *Mrs Brown's Boy's* scenario. Mary and Ken and others exist best on the airwaves and in the imagination. If they became flesh then our perception of Shuttleworth's world of carveries, ruffle bars and campervans would be shattered.

John Shuttleworth embodies elements of classic British comedy like Hancock, Del Boy and Harold Steptoe. You know that John will never leave his front room despite his aspirations.

I was flattered when Graham Fellows created a character based on my passions and flaws. Brian Appleton was a polytechnic music lecturer who was in effect the Zelig of British pop. He had unintentionally inspired everyone from Morrissey to Steve Harley, but had gained no recognition for this. In his own words Brian had been, 'Dumped on from a great height' by his famous counterparts. This character was launched in 1999 at The Pleasance Theatre in Edinburgh and Graham's integration of my Brummie tones and facial tics is flawless and frightening. They say imitation is the better part of flattery. It is. Ironically, in Graham's absence I had to deputise as Brian for Radio Scotland from a Newcastle studio - the producer didn't know quite what to think!

graham fellows inspired by chris phipps.

rbm comedy

eric burdon *bring it on home*

We Gotta Get Out Of This Place is a song that has had many lives and many interpretations. Written by Mann and Weill, it was originally demoed by The Righteous Brothers. In 2016 the only surviving Righteous Brother, Bill Medley, made his first British appearance as part of a nostalgia tour organised by David Gest. When he stepped on stage at Newcastle City Hall I felt that there was more than a touch of irony, not only had The Animals taken their potential hit and made it their own, but his and Bobby Hatfield's chart topper *Unchained Melody* had been re-interpreted (somewhat controversially) by Newcastle's Robson Green. I am amazed Bill Medley didn't think there was a conspiracy against him in the North East.

The voice of The Animals is of course Eric Burdon. As with all their finest songs, he delivers in a gritty collision of Geordie and American Blues twang. I travelled quite a long way for my first interview with Eric Burdon in 2001. I flew to Los Angeles and was driven to an adobe building seemingly in the middle of a desert, somewhere near Joshua Tree, I think. I stood in the heat, like a character in Film Noir, and there in the distance was

a line of rising dust. It was Eric, who arrived in true movie style on a vintage Harley Davidson. Like many vocalists he was daunting at first, in fact he definitely has an edge to him. After travelling thousands of miles I had one shot and I didn't want to get it wrong. The situation was defused when he offered to make me a cup of tea, while the cameraman who had driven me there set up the shots. Interviewing Eric was like a rollercoaster. He has done and survived so much that you never know quite where he is taking you with an answer, one minute he was telling me about bunking off college with future Animals' drummer John Steele to watch 'continental' films at The Stoll cinema in Newcastle, the next minute it's about meeting his idol Sam Cooke with his entourage on Grey Street. Inevitably, because they shared the same manager, he talked about Jimi Hendrix, who he claimed died with less than £10 in his bank account. When The Animals imploded Eric went to the record company accountants and asked for money that he was owed. The record company told him that it was *he* who owed *them* money! Not an unusual story in this business.

Eric Burdon has driven his own course as a highly resilient performer over the decades. The group that he formed post-Animals - War - were one of the first racially integrated rock bands, achieving a potent mix of blues, funk and jazz. *Eric Burdon Declares War* is a landmark album. In 2002, when he turned sixty-one, Eric played The Tyne Theatre and there were many faces there from his formative days at The Club A Go-Go.

I interviewed him aboard a boat cruising down the Tyne. As we passed under the Millenium Bridge he said, 'You know Jimi's got his rainbow bridge at last.' In 2018 Eric Burdon played the Theatre Royal in Newcastle to promote a fine new album. Like Mark Knopfler, he believes that the River Tyne and the Mississippi exist in parallel worlds. It was a river that gave him musical life. His 'Mississippi-on-Tyne' twang remains undiminished.

chris rea *hard is the road*

In the song *Rhinestone Cowboy*, Glen Campbell sang, 'There will be a load of compromising on the road to my horizon.' This was never the case for Teesside-born Chris Rea. Somebody once told me that it was the combination of grit and North winds that resulted in the unique vocal style and sound of the great Teesside trio of Paul Rodgers, David Coverdale and Chris Rea. Rea has pursued a fierce independence over the years. He was a late-comer to rock & roll, having toyed with the idea of joining the family ice cream business or being a journalist. When he heard the Delta blues coming out of an alarm clock radio that was it. He became a peerless slide guitarist and vocalist. It was as if the Delta had moved to the North East coast.

Because of his Italian parentage, his record company wanted to rename him Benny Santini and develop him into a clone of Elton John. Chris Rea's reaction has never been recorded, suffice to say he made an album called *Whatever Happened To Benny Santini?* developing a highly personalised mixture of gritty ballads and rock.

In 2003 I produced a documentary entitled *Hard Is The Road*. It was a personalised portrait of Chris centring on his then new album, *Songs From The Blue Cafe*. Like many performers, he prefers to speak through his music and is normally press and camera shy, but every artist if they have a product to sell, ultimately has to make themselves available. There are of course exceptions such as Prince and Bowie!

To break the ice with the interview I again searched for some common ground or experience. In his studio I had noticed a bust of the jazz trumpeter Miles Davis and an extraordinary box set of the legendary blues singer 'The Masked Marvel'- Charley Patton. The ground between us instantly unfroze because he discovered that, like him, I had a passion for both. In the interview he talked about how a life-threatening illness and undue pressures from the record company had completely changed the game for him. Now he had his own label and was able to tour and record to accommodate his health issues.

An interesting side effect of his illness had been that he had taken up art and his cover designs reflected that, as did the huge, colourful Picasso-esque canvases in the studio. He told me that he really knew that the public had taken him to heart when a national newspaper during petrol rationing ran a headline 'FUEL IF YOU THINK IT'S OVER.' This of course was a back reference to the song he had written for Elkie Brooks.

The two songs that really epitomise the North East for me are *Steel River* and *Windy Town*, of which there is a wonderful version by Rod Stewart.

The curious thing is that he is one of the few people that I have ever interviewed who talks about himself in the third person!

chris rea -
searching for the blue cafe.

alamy

ritchie blackmore *difficult to cure*

Robert 'Mutt' Lange, producer of AC/DC, Def Leppard and Shania Twain once said to me, 'I never give interviews because once you have been interviewed they've got you.'

This was clearly the philosophy adopted by Ritchie Blackmore, the uber-riffmeister who occupies the guitarist's Olympus, shared with Messrs. Page, Beck and Hendrix and the rest. Ritchie cut his teeth on the 1960s' British session scene, joining with another veteran, organist Jon Lord and Chris Curtis from The Searchers, evolving into a line-up that would become Deep Purple. Deep Purple were once listed as the loudest band on earth and Blackmore had a reputation for being both moody and creative. Deep Purple came to define hard rock with anthems like *Smoke On The Water*. When he tired of the funk direction the band were travelling in he formed Ritchie Blackmore's Rainbow who crossed over a rock sound into an AOR power ballad format, then, mercurial as ever, after reforming Deep Purple, he formed Blackmore's Night. This band was fronted by his wife, vocalist Candice Knight and he successfully pursued a fusion of Medieval, Tudor and hard rock, with a lot of other influences thrown in. Some critics were initially derisory - but it worked impeccably.

Ritchie Blackmore was enigmatic, a perfectionist

and a practical joker on a par with Orson Welles. Members of his bands would often find that their hotel room on tour had been completely redecorated! In 1971, at the California Jam, he rammed his guitar neck directly into the camera lens on stage, one of the greatest shots of all time. Unsurprisingly, he rarely gave interviews. In the 70s I took over the rock show on BBC Radio Birmingham. One night the duty engineer told me that there was a Mr Blackmore on the phone. I couldn't believe it. It was however, not Blackmore the guitarist, it was a youth employment officer - my hopes were dashed!

In 2013, the promoter for Newcastle's Tyne Theatre, Jim Semmence told me that he had booked Blackmore's Night and that Ritchie was up for an interview by phone from New York. On the day of the interview I was told that he was not now available and that it was his wife Candice who would do the interview. I went ahead, and when I rang her Ritchie was actually there. I realise now that this was a test. If I had said I was only interested in him he would never have taken part-mischievous as ever. One of the most interesting parts of the interview was about his early years with Screaming Lord Sutch and The Savages of which he was one. He told me he was required to cavort about in leopard skin briefs but that it was a sobering lesson in stagecraft that would serve him well. When he was in The Outlaws, with bassist Chas Hodges (of future 'geezers' Chas and Dave), and on tour with The Rolling Stones, he would catch Keith Richards peering from the side of the stage to see how he was playing.

Some months after the interview I found myself at Lumley Castle near Chester-le-Street where there was a press junket for Blackmore's Night. Prior to the performance and a medieval banquet we were given a conducted tour of the castle. Our guide was dressed as a monk and we were taken into the cellars where we were suddenly plunged into darkness and a disembodied voice announced, 'You don't think you've got away with it that easily do you?' I was waiting for trapdoors to be opened or something nasty to be poured over us but fortunately it didn't happen and we were released to enjoy the concert. We were all presented with a small cauldron containing a red candle. It didn't explode! Unpredictable as ever, Blackmore has reformed Rainbow to great acclaim.

ritchie blackmore - 'are you looking at me?'

alamy

pet shop boys *the conundrum*

No 'The Conundrum' is not their new album title, it summarises the situation I was faced with when producing a documentary of The Pet Shop Boys' performance of *Battleship Potemkin* in Wallsend on Tyne in 2006.

Battleship Potemkin is one of the greatest films of all time. It tells of a naval mutiny in Tsarist Russia. The climax, where innocent people are slaughtered on the Odessa Steps, is a masterpiece of editing. It was in fact imitated by Brian De Palma in the movie *The Untouchables*. That shape-shifting pop duo The Pet Shop Boys devised a score to accompany this silent landmark and it had been successfully staged in London. Now it was to be performed in the enormous dry dock of the Swan Hunter shipyard. The Northern Sinfonia based at Sage Gateshead, would accompany The Pet Shop Boys live on a specially built stage. They would be dwarfed by the walls of the dock and a hospital ship that was being fitted out there.

It was without doubt the coldest outdoor location I have ever experienced. A high wind blew down the Tyne and promptly demolished all the music stands and sheet music during rehearsals. The concrete and stone surroundings made everything seem even icier than they were. We might as well have stood in a wind tunnel that tested jet engines.

The biggest problem was not the climate, but the production. When a movie is shown on television rights have to be cleared and paid for. In the case of Russian classics Glasnost had rendered them public domain or in dispute. The fact that *Potemkin* was given as a freebie with a Sunday paper showed at the time that it was public domain. The real problem was with the music. If I synchronised The Pet Shop Boys' score with the screened movie, as in the concert, it would be classified as a full blown televisual soundtrack performance with huge financial implications. If you watch the production, which was called *The Yards*, the film doesn't match with the music but you think it does. This illusion was all down to the highly skilled editing of Fiona Toal.

I found it quite amusing that Neil and Chris had to don construction hard hats. They looked as though they had joined The Village People.

'the village people - us?'

mirrorpix

jon lord soundtrack of the cathedral city

Of all the photographs in this book, this one deserves a caption. I like to think that Jon Lord is asking me whether I would be interested in joining Deep Purple. The occasion was the launch of his album *Durham Concerto*, which was his orchestrated musical homage to that venerable city and cathedral. It was essentially his original soundtrack for the sequence of city, cathedral and student life.

Unknowingly, I had booked Jon Lord for a school gig in the 1960s. He was then a member of the band The Artwoods, who were fronted by Ronnie Wood's brother. They brought out an EP entitled *Jazz in Jeans*, which is now highly collectable. During the interview in Durham, he told me that as an aspiring session musician he even found himself backing the Flower Pot Men! Of course, as many great session men coming up through the ranks and the burgeoning studio scene in the 60s, he would eventually found one of the world's great rock bands, Deep Purple. One of the iconic onstage trademarks of Deep Purple on stage

was Jon Lord's Hammond organ battling Ritchie Blackmore's lead guitar. In 2002 he quit Deep Purple to pursue his first love, which was classical composition. He explained that it was still difficult as a rock musician to be taken seriously as a classical composer. Even when he was rehearsing in the cathedral there was pressure for him to trot out a few bars from *Smoke on the Water*. The most significant thing he said to me was that when you buy a ticket for a band concert you both enter into a contract - for the band that means turning up and performing to the best of their ability. On a more humorous note, certain visitors to the cathedral that day thought he was Roger Whittaker, the composer of *Durham Town*, possibly because they both sported white beards and spectacles. As an aside, it is interesting to note that *Durham Town* was written by Roger Whittaker as a bet prior to the Michael Aspel Show. Charming though it is, it is geographically incorrect as the River Tyne is mentioned only because it rhymed, unlike the River Wear which flows through Durham.

jon lord asks me to be in deep purple - 2007.

mike hodges *you're a big man, but...*

I first saw *Get Carter* on its release in 1971 at the Forum cinema in New Street, Birmingham. Along with Sidney Lumet's *The Pawnbroker*, it had quite an impact on me. Eleven years later, like Jack Carter, I found myself on a train bound for Newcastle. I was determined to emulate Michael Caine and order a drink at the very pub he calls in at when he gets off the train. I of course went to the wrong pub which is now called The Head of Steam. Unbeknown to me, the actual location known as the Long Bar was long gone and had become Dante Piero's pizza restaurant. I can't see Jack walking in there.

Many people's image of the North East has been heavily influenced, somewhat controversially, by *Get Carter* and it inspired me to make a documentary and write a book about the cultural stereotyping and cinematic history of the region.

In 2011, to celebrate the 40th anniversary of *Get Carter*, I found myself interviewing its director Mike Hodges on a Carter-themed bus tour organised by Tyne Idols Heritage Tour Company. Also on board the bus was actor Alun Armstrong, one of our greatest character actors whose first film appearance was as Keith in *Get Carter*. He and Hodges had not met since 1971.

During the interview I discovered that the film was made in Newcastle almost by default. Mike Hodges not only directed but also wrote the screenplay from Ted Lewis's original novel *Jack's Return Home*. This was located in Lewis's home area of Hull and Scunthorpe. Mike Hodges drove to reconnoitre that area and didn't find it suitable. He then remembered the Tyneside Coast from his days on board a minesweeper. When he took a taxi across Newcastle and saw the buildings that were physically and *politically* changing its skyline he knew that this was the city that Jack Carter would return to for vengeance. It is down to Mike Hodges that *Get Carter* remains undated with its gritty urban authenticity and violence. Ironically, the film didn't develop its following and credibility until twenty years later, in fact Hodges told me that for him *Get Carter* was like a cinematic message in a bottle, it took two decades to have full impact.

There is a humorous footnote. The iconic scene in the film is when Carter throws corrupt businessman Cliff Brumby off the Gateshead car park, a concrete tower of Babel. It is alleged to be a multi storey example of 'concrete brutalism' and was a constant source of lobbying by film preservationists who tried to prevent its destruction. Eventually it bit the dust and the concrete, whilst fans made off with souvenir chunks.

One of these concrete artefacts was presented to Mike Hodges to celebrate his RTS. Lifetime

Achievement Award. As he received the souvenir it looked rather heavy. I didn't know whether the weight of it would make him fall off or disappear through the stage. Fortunately he kept his balance, though he looked shocked at the weight of the award.

Mike is still on good form and was back in Newcastle in 2018 for its first International Film Festival. Thankfully there aren't any parts of the car park left.

alun armstrong, *get carter* director mike hodges and chris phipps on the tyne idols bus tour 2011.

diane phipps

roger daltrey *don't get fooled again*

I interviewed Roger Daltrey twice and the interviews were separated by forty years. The subject of both was the movie *Tommy*. The first interview was when the film was released in 1975 at BBC Radio Birmingham at Pebble Mill. As with all major radio interviews I was supplied with production notes and biographies for the film and four decades later I still had them - maybe I knew they would come in handy and they did!

Whitley Bay Film Festival is organised by Ema Lea Daggett and Simon Fitzpatrick. The festival patron, who is incredibly supportive, is Ian La Frenais. Under the auspices of The Teenage Cancer Trust, the festival secured an exclusive appearance by Roger Daltrey in 2015. A good thing I had kept the notes!

The interview took place at a packed Whitley Bay Playhouse. In the dressing room Roger Daltrey was bemused by the fact that I still had the original production notes and was pleased that a newly signed copy would be auctioned later that night for the Trust. Inevitably there is always a tension between interviewer and guest prior to the event. You have to gauge what might be off limits. I detected he was not too happy with a film recently released about The Who's original managers Lambert and Stamp, so I avoided it. This episode regarding the notes broke the ice between us and the interview went ahead after Roger had been given a standing ovation. I felt we could have talked for much longer as he was clearly enjoying himself. A major interview like this is like driving a fast car, you have to split your attention between what is being said and at the same time mentally edit the proceedings for the next question and keep it on track and look at your watch!

At the end of the interview he confounded his minders by jumping into the audience and signing autographs.

A footnote: *Tommy* along with another Daltrey movie was directed by the auteur Ken Russell. Russell had a reputation for visually stunning, highly erotic movies, many of them about musicians like Tchaichovsky, Mahler and Liszt. His film *The Devils* caused a storm of controversy and his *Women In Love* is seen as definitive. Unbelievably, Ken Russell was offered *Summer Holiday*, about the exploits of Cliff Richard and his youthful pals on the continent. He turned it down. Just think what might have happened if he had said yes. What would have taken place on that bus? We will never know.

roger daltrey at whitley bay playhouse, 2015.

george bosnyak/whitley bay film festival

pete docherty *the libertine*

Many years ago, as a teenager, I saw a war veteran sinking a pint of beer, sat on a step of a city centre public house in Birmingham. It was an extraordinary site because he had detached his prosthetic leg and placed it in the gutter, so there he was, dissociated from his own limb - if only I had had a camera on that occasion.

Pete Docherty was a contradiction, walking the fine line between making powerful music and blatant self-destruction. In the early 2000s I had just completed filming in central London and was walking along Denmark Street, the traditional centre of London's music business. Here, Rock & Roll had come crawling out of basement clubs in the 1950s. As I paused on the street, I became aware of a rather dilapidated Jaguar saloon shadowing me. The sunroof was open and surveying the scene, rather like a papal visit, was Pete Docherty. He could see I was accompanied by a freelance cameraman and asked me what I was up to. He clearly thought that we were news paparazzi, as he was on everybody's news hit list at that time. Being spontaneous and opportunistic, I decided to ask him whether he would be interested in talking to me about the pitfalls of the music business. We had quite a warm, brief conversation and he handed me an address hastily written on a piece of paper. This time I had a camera with me.

I had to take a train out of London, so was never able to do the interview, but the image really captures that moment where all the stars literally align to give you a perfect picture. There is Pete Docherty, his hat at a jaunty angle, rather like a Soho wide boy, aligned with the words in neon 'Tin Pan Alley!' One picture that says it all

a time in place in sync.

the unlikely lads

Dick Clement and Ian La Frenais revolutionised television comedy in the 1960s. Out went 'drawing room' farce and in came *The Likely Lads*, Bob and Terry, freewheeling with their disposable income in a post-war Northern England. Clement and La Frenais went on to create inimitable characters like Fletcher (*Porridge*) and Oz (*Auf Wiedersehen, Pet*) and many other tragi-comic figures in the landscapes of our lives and times. Their talent doesn't stop here, the duo have written or adapted material for big screen blockbusters, stage and animation.

I have interviewed Dick and Ian three times. The first interview happened by default. They had been recruited by AC/DC lead singer Brian Johnson to write the book of a stage musical initially entitled *Helen of Troy*. Brian was writing this with another great Northern entertainer Brendan Healey and together they were structuring songs around one of the most famous mythological tales. Brian is a man of extraordinary energy and once he starts on a project there are few that can resist him. He told me that if I turned up with a film crew at a studio in the Van Nuys suburb of Los Angeles that I would have the basis of a potential documentary about the 'Helen' project. I turned up at the studio to find Clement and La Frenais, Meatloaf's lead guitarist, backing singers and the venerable actor Malcolm

McDowell who were rehearsing a number newly completed by Brian and Brendan entitled *It's Good To Be God*. As you can imagine I did a lot of interviews that day. McDowell was going to play Zeus - he told me this was an improvement on playing Caligula, who after all was only a man who thought he was a god *and* he'd get to keep his clothes on. I interviewed Dick and Ian in their office and they told me that their ultimate ambition as writers was to get a track on an AC/DC album. I find that their great quality is their generosity. They have an acute sense and love of music, humanity and the vagaries of entertainment which you find in their movies like *The Commitments*, *Still Crazy* and most recently the Michael Caine presented documentary on the 60s' class and cultural revolution in London, *My Generation*. At the time of writing Dick and Ian have a musical and a play due to open in Canada and London respectively.

Ian La Frenais' generosity extends to his personal patronage of The Whitley Bay Film Festival, an extraordinary community arts event now in its ninth year. One of the most memorable moments was interviewing Ian about a Clement and La Frenais movie that in my opinion has been criminally ignored, and I think they feel that as well. *Across The Universe*, as you might guess, is a Beatles project directed by Julie Taymor. As writers, they structured a love story around thirty-four Beatles' compositions. It is the tale of star-crossed lovers Jude and Lucy and it spans the political and generational upheavals of the time when the songs were written. A mixture of live and animated action, it is inexplicable why this movie hasn't been seen by the audience it deserves. Even the names of Clement and La Frenais and cameo appearances by the likes of Bono and Joe Cocker didn't guarantee success at the box office – entertainment is a fickle business. Ian has a sardonic sense of humour and a mischievous edge that always puts me on my mettle when I interview him but I rather enjoy this - no room for complacency.

I am convinced that Ian's earliest script efforts were for a local TV advertising magazine programme called *Ned's Shed*. He vehemently denies this!

with dick clement and ian la frenais, the exchange, north shields, 2018.

dave turnbull/whitley bay film festival

the management *regrets nothing*

Inevitably, being involved in broadcasting in the 70s and 80s, I would come into contact with moguls of the music business, particularly those involved in music publishing and management, after all I might be of some use to them. Many of these extraordinary characters had a trademark uniform - expensive and colourful sports jackets. Maybe they all bought them from the same tailor.

Once I found myself at lunch with one of the most powerful music publishers in the world, Freddy Bienstock. Bienstock to me was most famous for being the go-to publisher for Elvis Presley, whom he had signed to RCA records. For over ten years Elvis went to him exclusively for his choice of songs. Freddy told me that one day Elvis unexpectedly came to him with a song. It was an Italian ballad *O Sole Mio*, and he asked Bienstock to obtain an English language version. It became of course *It's Now Or Never.*

It was quite an extraordinary conversation. He confided in me that coming from a Country & Western publishing background he was initially unsure about Rock & Roll and its future, as, prior to Elvis, he had been dealing with country artists like Hank Snow and Eddie Arnold.

He had spent his life acquiring song collections from everyone from U2 to Michael Jackson, and supplying songs to clients like Cliff Richard. His publishing company, named [in a fashion] after his daughter, was Carlin Music. We talked about the artists who had covered *Fever*, including Peggy Lee and I told him that I loved the original version by an R&B singer called Little Willie John. This seemed to impress him and he complemented me that I reminded him of Seymour Stein, the co-founder of Sire Records. What Mr. Stein and I had in common I have never discovered though he was described as the 'edgy cat who signed the Ramones'. Bienstock's final confession to me was that on the way to the lunch he had stopped off in Venice and bought a Canaletto - no wonder he had a flash sports jacket!

The other memory of a loud garment was a one-off meeting with the 'enfant terrible' of music management Andrew Oldham. He of course managed The Rolling Stones and owned Immediate Records, the home of The Small Faces, Chris Farlowe etc. I had come up with an idea for a Channel 4 programme called *The Management Regrets Nothing*. The idea was that Oldham would visit infamous and famous music managers and engage them in conversations about their tricks of the trade and anecdotes about their client relationships. I met with him and his business partner Tony Calder in an exclusive gentlemen's club in Chelsea. For some reason the actor David

Warner, reading a book, kept walking in and out of the lounge while we were talking. Oldham and Calder were quite up for the idea and suggested demonstrating management techniques such as hanging people out of windows by their ankles. Oldham was wearing a jacket I can only describe as ostentatious and he spontaneously burst into song - Sinatra numbers if I remember rightly. He told me that fame was seizing the moment as it passed in front of you and the ability to be mentally and physically screwed by it. He said Brian Jones of The Rolling Stones could never accept it. He told me that they had recorded Page and Clapton in his front room jamming on numbers called *Tail Dragger* and *Tribute to Elmore* - you can find them on any budget compilation today but were on the *Immediate British Blues Anthology*.

However promising a programme proposal can be, it doesn't necessarily get made. This fascinating premise never got beyond one commissioning meeting. I believe Andrew Oldham now lives deep in the jungles of Bogota like a Rock & Roll version of the Colonel in *Apocalypse Now*.

alan klein and andrew oldham - 'i've got the beatles and you've got the stones.'

james brown *let a man come in*

I thought I would finish with a story which is an exception to everything else in this book - how I *almost* met James Brown.

James Brown was known by many monikers - the most famous were 'The Godfather of Soul' and 'The Hardest Working Man in Show Business'. The latter nickname came from his tireless tour schedules across the world and his relentless recording output. James Brown transformed his early brand of classic soul and R&B and in many ways invented and innovated Funk. He brought to it gravity-defying dance moves which were only ever equalled by Prince. Brown had the tightest band on the planet - the Famous Flames - and his stage shows were spectacularly over the top. Before the encores, The Godfather would fake physical collapse on stage and his MC would cover him in a cloak upon which, like Lazarus, he would rise again to perform yet another song.

The Tube opened in 1982 with the last performance by The Jam. Now, five years later, it looked as though James Brown would bring the final series to a spectacular conclusion. It took nearly two months negotiating through a Swiss promoter to bring James Brown to Newcastle as part of his European tour.

Surprisingly, the financial side was not too daunting as the act would accept musician union scale payments. However, other demands were more eccentric. Firstly, I was told that Mr Brown would only stay in a presidential suite in Newcastle. The nearest I could get was in the Gosforth Park Hotel where, as I explained to his management, Bruce Springsteen and Queen had stayed. Retrospectively, they must have thought that I had said *the* Queen had been a hotel guest and they agreed straight away. Then there was the problem of air transport. James Brown used private planes and did not sit with the band. On this occasion they had to accept that there was no first class on the London to Newcastle shuttle only Coach Class. I did however succeed in getting British Airways to draw a curtain between James Brown and the band during the flight. I also anticipated problems during the performance. I was told that the Famous Flames didn't sound check, they would walk on stage to positions marked in chalk and actually sound check during the first number. My main worry was that the MC's introduction to James Brown, where he and the band wound the audience up for twenty minutes, would take so long that programme would actually finish before he got into an actual number!

Three days before the gig, James Brown cancelled due to dental problems which were affecting his singing. In the end the last band to perform on *The Tube* in 1987 were Duran Duran who were flown in from Belfast by EMI at the last minute. They gave a powerhouse performance, particularly of new numbers like *Skin Trade* and they had a new line up including Steve Ferrone on drums.

I was naturally disappointed that James Brown didn't make it, because he was far more than a performer. Apart from his music, James Brown had successful businesses which made him an inspiration to black entrepreneurs. He in fact carried on unfinished work initiated by earlier positive black showbiz role models such as Sam Cooke and Otis Redding before their untimely exits. I also feel that James Brown does not get credit for some of the world's worst record sleeve designs -maybe no one ever dared to tell him? Just look at *It's a Man's World*. It's a no-brainer.

soul brother no. 1.

125

errol flynn ozymandias

I took this photograph in the Hollywood hills. It reminds me of the poem *Ozymandias*, which deals with the passage of time and greatness. The steps you see led into Errol Flynn's Hollywood mansion. The glitterati of Hollywood once stood and probably fell on these steps. This picture to me makes a statement about fame and mortality and I leave you to draw your own conclusions.

epilogue

What goes around comes around. In 2018 I was hosting the opening event for Whitley Bay Film Festival. This involved an interview with the legendary Black Sabbath guitarist Tony Iommi. The way that he and his band have been perceived over the decades is a salutary lesson in the law of the entertainment business.

In the early seventies Black Sabbath were adored by fans, hated by the press; in the eighties, when I was involved with *The Tube* they were regarded as uncool. Ozzy, however, became credible through reality TV, then with their thirteenth album they were at number one again and vindicated by everyone from Nirvana to Metallica. It is this rollercoaster of attitudes, chance and credibility that has always fascinated me and will continue to do so. My interviewees fascinate me even more.

In 2018 I had the mixed accolade of appearing on the *Antiques Roadshow* 40th Anniversary, broadcast from Newcastle. It wasn't me that was being valued it was my collection.

The last word goes to my friend, the late Black Country poet Jim William Jones. They summarise feelings about my Midland roots and indirectly about the music which came from that Black Country area of the West Midlands...

From under the smoke,
The song of the people swells,
elemental as an old hymn.
Rising with the traffic of souls.
Their triumph spins around the world,
Wherever talk of fire and steel.
Inspires the muscle and the will of men,
whose altars reek of power.
The bursting channels of the sun
Have washed their offspring,
And the speckled universe,
Has felt the beating of their hearts.

Jim William Jones

(the black country society)

the loneliness of the long-distance interviewer.

ie phipps

clockwise from top left) 1. DJing in 1968. 2. with helicopter for the tube when budgets were big, cannes, 1983.
3. last episode of look! hear! with toyah willcox. 4. with alan clayson and denny laine (moody blues) at
northumbria university, 1994. 5. ann and nancy wilson of heart, 1986.

diane phipps

diane phipps

clockwise from top left) 1. looking cool. 2. interviewing uber-director dick carruthers at bradford.
3. interviewing mark knopfler at air studios, 1993. 4. with rainbow vocalist graham bonnet, le mondrian, 1986.
5. with roger daltrey, 2016.

steve bro

chris phipps
*name*dropper!